# INCREDIBLE PROTECTION

## AMID TURBULENCES

LESLIE M. JOHN

# INCREDIBLE PROTECTION

# AMID TURBULENCES

# LESLIE M. JOHN

**DESCRIPTON:**

This book brings out marvelous ways God uses to protect His children. Not every method God uses to protect and deliver His children is similar to the other. Every method differs from the other. It includes the fall of kings Nebuchadnezzar and Belshazzar, and God's protection of Daniel, Shadrach, Meshach and Abednego.

**ABOUT THE AUTHOR:**

The author, who accepted Lord Jesus Christ as his personal Savior when he was a boy of 13, was raised in a Christian family and had education in Christian Institutions.

This then was the message that he heard of the Son of God, Lord Jesus Christ. This then is the message that he declares that God is light and in Him there is no darkness at all. Jesus Christ is the Son of God sent from above to save sinners.

Jesus died on the cross bearing our sins upon Himself. He was buried and God raised Him on the third day. Jesus, after having appeared to many for 40 days ascended to heaven. He will come again. Whosoever confesses his/her sins to Him and believe in heart that God raised Him from the dead will not perish but will have everlasting life.

"Jesus saith unto him, I am the way, the truth, and the life: no man cometh unto the Father, but by me" (John 14:6).

Scriptures quoted in this book are from KJV from open domain, and from NIV, ESV, and NLT not greater than the number permitted.

Holy Bible, New International Version®, NIV® Copyright ©1973, 1978, 1984, 2011 by Biblica, Inc. ® Used by permission. All rights reserved worldwide.

The Holy Bible, English Standard Version. ESV® Permanent Text Edition® (2016). Copyright © 2001 by Crossway Bibles, a publishing ministry of Good News Publishers.

ISBN-10:0-9985181-1-5
ISBN-13:978-0-9985181-1-4

# CONTENTS

INCREDIBLE PROTECTION ....................................................1

    AMID TURBULENCES.................................................1

CONTENTS.......................................................................4

CHAPTER 1 BE STRONG AND OF  GOOD COURAGE ..............7

CHAPTER 2 COMFORTING VERSES ......................................9

CHAPTER 3 GOD PROTECTS HIS CHILDREN .........................11

CHAPTER 4 UNCONDITIONAL COVENANT..........................15

CHAPTER 5 NO WEAPON SHALL PROSPER .........................18

CHAPTER 6 THE LAND OF GOSHEN...................................21

CHAPTER 7 THE LORD ANSWERS PRAYERS ........................25

CHAPTER 8 THE PLAGUES IN EGYPT ..................................28

    THE THREE SIGNS .................................................28

    ONLY ONE SIGN WAS SHOWN ...............................29

    PLAGUE - DEFINITION ...........................................29

CHAPER 9 THE PLAGUES ..................................................30

    PLAGUE 1:  RIVER NILE TURNED INTO BLOOD ................30

    PLAGUE 2: THE PLAGUE OF FROGS ................................30

    PLAUGE 3: THE PLAGUE OF LICE................................30

    PLAGUE 4: THE PLAGUE OF FLIES .................................30

    PLAGUE 5: THE PLAGUE O F MURRAIN..........................30

    PLAGUE 6: THE PLAGUE OF BOILS AND BLAINS .............30

    PLAUGE 7: THE PLAGUE OF HAIL .................................31

    PLAGUE 8: THE PLAGUE OF LOCUSTS ............................31

PLAUGE 9: THE PLAGUE OF DARKNESS ..........................31

PLAGUE 10: THE FIRSTBORN KILLED ..............................31

GOD COULD HAVE STARTED IT ALL OVER AGAIN ..............34

CHAPTER 11 OUR BLESSINGS IN ABRAHAM ........................37

ABRAHAM OBEYED ................................................38

ABRAHAM'S FAITH ...............................................38

THE BLESSING OF ABRAHAM ...........................................39

CHAPTER 12 SARAH RESCUED...................................41

CHAPTER 13 REBEKAH RESCUED ...............................44

CHAPTER 14 ABRAHAM SEEKS ANSWERS ........................45

CHAPTER 15 TRIUMPHANT HEZEKIAH ...............................46

GOD BLESSED HEZEKIAH .........................................54

CHAPTER 16 DANIEL'S FOOD CHOICE ...............................56

CHAPTER 17 NEBUCHADNEZZAR'S DREAM .........................59

CHAPTER 18 THE FOLLY OF IDOLATRY ...............................72

CHAPTER 19 NEBUCHADNEZZAR HUMBLED ......................78

CHAPTER 20 NEBUCHADNEZZAR HUMILIATED..................83

CHAPTER 21 NEBUCHADNEZZAR RESTORED ....................85

CHAPTER 22 HAUGHTY BELSHAZZAR HUMBLED ...............87

CHAPTER 23 DANIEL'S COMFORT AMID LIONS ..................92

PRAY FOR THE RULERS...........................................98

LORD JESUS SAID... .............................................99

CHAPTER 24 GOD PROVIDES ....................................100

CHAPTER 25 PAUL COMFORTS ..................................107

CHAPTER 26 APOSTLE PAUL RESCUED ...............................110

CHAPTER 27 JESUS REBUKES STORMS.......................116

CHAPTER 28 THE SUPERIORITY OF CHRIST.......................120

CHAPER 29 PARTAKERS OF HEAVENLY CALLING .............123

CHAPTER 30 THE MISSION OF JESUS ...................................127

   HAS GOD CASTAWAY THE CHILDREN OF ISRAEL? No! ..127

CHAPTER 31 REDEEMED BY HIS BLOOD .............................129

CHAPTER 32 INTERCESSORY PRAYER...................................131

   THE INTERCESSORY PRAYER OF LORD JESUS CHRIST ..132

CHAPTER 33 THE SAME SPIRITUAL DRINK ..........................134

CHAPTER 34 OUR HAIR ARE NUMBERED .............................138

CHATER 35 POOR PROTECTED .............................................142

CHAPTER 36 ALL FOR GOOD.................................................145

CHAPTER 37 HEIR OF ALL THINGS ......................................149

CHAPTER 38 A BETER COVENANT ........................................152

CHAPTER 39 ROYAL PRIESTHOOD ........................................157

CHAPTER 40 LIVING SACRIFICE.............................................162

# CHAPTER 1
# BE STRONG AND OF
# GOOD COURAGE

"Be strong and of a good courage: for unto this people shalt thou divide for an inheritance the land, which I swore unto their fathers to give them". Joshua 1:6

Standing on the banks of Jordan River Joshua spoke at length to the children of Israel. Joshua was the successor of Moses in leadership to take them to the Promised Land Canaan. Moses failed in an incident, which in the sight of God was a serious matter, because it was equivalent to dishonoring God. God told Moses to speak to the rock, which would then produce water for the thirsty Israelites, but Moses struck the rock.

Moses thought it was right to do so because God said to Him in an earlier occasion to strike the rock to get water. Inasmuch as Moses failed to do just as God told him to do God said to him that he will not enter the Promised Land, Canaan; nevertheless he would be able to see it from afar.

The Lord said to Joshua... "This book of the law shall not depart out of thy mouth; but thou shalt meditate therein day and night, that thou may observe to do according to all that is written therein: for then thou shalt make thy way prosperous, and then thou shalt have good success". Joshua 1:8

Joshua spoke to the children of God, the Israelites, and advised them to be courageous and not to be afraid. The spies who went out earlier to search the land of Canaan came with disappointing news that the people in Canaan were giants.

Joshua instilled courage in the minds of the children of Israel and advised them to meditate on God's word every day and every night.

"And they answered Joshua, saying, All that thou command us we will do, and whithersoever thou send us, we will go" (Joshua 1:16)

It is imperative that we meditate on the Word of God every day, in order grow in the Lord and to keep Satan away from us. If we allow Satan to enter our hearts, we will certainly backslide. Jesus asserts here that he is the good shepherd, who will not let his sheep be stolen by his enemy. He would leave ninety nine sheep aside for some time to go in search of one lost or backslidden sheep to bring it back to join the ninety nine.

"I am the good shepherd, and know my sheep, and am known of mine". John 10:14

"My sheep hear my voice, and I know them, and they follow me: And I give unto them eternal life; and they shall never perish, neither shall any man pluck them out of my hand. My Father, which gave them me, is greater than all; and no man is able to pluck them out of my Father's hand. I and my Father are one". John 10:27-30

# CHAPTER 2
# COMFORTING VERSES

*Be strong and of a good courage, fear not, nor be afraid of them: for the LORD thy God, he it is that doth go with thee; he will not fail thee, nor forsake thee. (Deuteronomy 31:6)*

*For ye have not received the spirit of bondage again to fear; but ye have received the Spirit of adoption, whereby we cry, Abba, Father. (Romans 8:15)*

*And because ye are sons, God hath sent forth the Spirit of his Son into your hearts, crying, Abba, Father. (Galatians 4:6)*

*"For he hath made him to be sin for us, who knew no sin; that we might be made the righteousness of God in him" (2 Corinthians 5:21)*

*"I pray not that thou shouldest take them out of the world, but that thou shouldest keep them from the evil. They are not of the world, even as I am not of the world". (John 17:15-16)*

*"Sanctify them through thy truth: thy word is truth. As thou hast sent me into the world, even so have I also sent them into the world. And for their sakes I sanctify myself, that they also might be sanctified through the truth". (John 17:17-19)*

*"I pray not that thou shouldest take them out of the world, but that thou shouldest keep them from the evil. They are not of the world, even as I am not of the world". (John 17:15-16)*

*Jesus was not saying in His prayer that His disciples should be moved out from this world to safe havens, but He prayed that they may be kept safe from the evil. He testified that even as the Lord was not of this world, they were also not of the world.*

*"And such were some of you: but ye are washed, but ye are sanctified, but ye are justified in the name of the Lord Jesus, and by the Spirit of our God". (1 Corinthians 6:11)*

# CHAPTER 3
# GOD PROTECTS HIS CHILDREN

When God decided to protect his precious ones whom He considered are upright and his followers he called them into a secure place, before destroying the wicked ones who rejected Him.

Noah, who was just and perfect in the sight of God, walked with Him Therefore, God moved Noah and his family into the Ark a secure place, while he poured out His wrath on those who rejected Him. Thus, Noah and his family were saved from the wrath of God.

In a similar way when God pours out His wrath against those who rejected him as their Savior, He protects the Church and keep the believers away from his wrath. He saved them from destruction. He grants them eternal life to be with Him always. (Genesis 6:9, Genesis 7:16 and 1 Thessalonians 4:17). Surely the indignation shown by those who rejected Jesus as their Messiah will be paid for while those who are saved and protected are asked to be patient until He deals with them in His wrath.

"Come, my people, enter thou into thy chambers, and shut thy doors about thee: hide thyself as it were for a little moment, until the indignation be over past. For, behold, the LORD cometh out of his place to punish the inhabitants of the earth for their iniquity: the earth also shall disclose her blood, and shall no more cover her slain". (Isaiah 26:20-21)

The comfort and security provided to the believers in Christ is seen in Zephaniah 2:3 where the prophet calls for repentance in order that they may be saved and hid during the period of

Lord's anger. The prophet asks them to seek the LORD and His righteousness, and meekness in order that they may be hid in the day of the LORD's anger.

Speaking to Jewish audience Jesus warned them not to be taken away by enticing words of anyone who would say that here is Christ or there! He said many will come in His name and will teach false doctrines and prophesy false. He said Antichrist, the son of perdition, will call himself as Christ.

Jesus said to them to be careful and not believe him because the Son of man will come as a lightening out of the east, and shines even unto the west.

"Wherefore if they shall say unto you, Behold, he is in the desert; go not forth: behold, he is in the secret chambers; believe it not. For as the lightning cometh out of the east, and shines even unto the west; so shall also the coming of the Son of man be. For wheresoever the carcass is, there will the eagles be gathered together". (Matthew 24:26-28)

John saw in his vision a great multitude whom no one could number. They were from all nations and they stood before the throne of the Lamb. He saw that a great voice from heaven called those who are saved to "Come up hither" and they ascended up to heaven in a cloud while their enemies watched them.

Those who were caught up were from all nations, kindred, and people of all tongues and they stood before the throne of the Lamb, clothed in white robes, and palms in their hands. (Revelation 7:9, Revelation 11:12)

The man child in Revelation represented Lord Jesus Christ in whose blood our sins are cleansed. The loud voice said that the salvation, the kingdom of our God and the power of Christ is come. The accuser, Satan, who is also called the great dragon, that old serpent, the Devil, who deceived Eve in the Garden of Eden, was cast out into the earth along with his fellow evil angels.

Those who were overcome by the blood of the Lamb were saved and are asked to rejoice. It will be the time when Satan who will have very little time pursues and persecutes the nation of Israel during the Great Tribulation period.

"And the great dragon was cast out, that old serpent, called the Devil, and Satan, which deceiveth the whole world: he was cast out into the earth, and his angels were cast out with him. And I heard a loud voice saying in heaven, Now is come salvation, and strength, and the kingdom of our God, and the power of his Christ: for the accuser of our brethren is cast down, which accused them before our God day and night. And they overcame him by the blood of the Lamb, and by the word of their testimony; and they loved not their lives unto the death. Therefore rejoice, ye heavens, and ye that dwell in them. Woe to the inhabiters of the earth and of the sea! for the devil is come down unto you, having great wrath, because he knoweth that he hath but a short time. And when the dragon saw that he was cast unto the earth, he persecuted the woman which brought forth the man child". (Revelation 12:9-13)

Jesus himself said that he will come in the clouds of heaven with power of great glory and then all the tribes of the earth mourn and they shall see his coming. It is at that time that he shall send his angels with great sound of trumpet and they shall 'gather together his elect from the four winds, from one end of heaven to the other'(Mathew 24:30, 31).

John also saw in his vision the Son of man coming in the cloud with a golden crown on his head. 'And he that sat on the cloud thrust in his sickle on the earth; and the earth was reaped'

"And I looked, and behold a white cloud, and upon the cloud one sat like unto the Son of man, having on his head a golden crown, and in his hand a sharp sickle. And another angel came out of the temple, crying with a loud voice to him that sat on the cloud, Thrust in thy sickle, and reap: for the time is come for thee to reap; for the harvest of the earth is ripe. And he that sat on the cloud thrust in his sickle on the earth; and the earth was reaped". (Revelation 14:14-16)

# CHAPTER 4
# UNCONDITIONAL COVENANT

"And he said unto him, I am the LORD that brought thee out of Ur of the Chaldees, to give thee this land to inherit it" (Genesis 15:7)

Beliefs and passions run very high and deep in the land of Israel because it is the land of three great faiths – Judaism, Christianity and Islam. The history of Israel is so complicated and contentious and, therefore, as Christians, it is apt that we depend on what is recorded in the Bible rather than any history book.

The whole of land of Israel is said to be not greater than New Jersey or even half of Georgia State where I live, yet the land of Israel is known to have suffered with wars and disputes. The disputes can be traced back even unto the days of Abraham, who was also known as 'father Abraham' by all the three faiths. Abraham's name was "Abram" before he was renamed by God as "Abraham".

A covenant is a mutual agreement between two parties and it is deemed to have agreed upon when both the parties pass between the divided pieces of an animal that are laid against each other indicating that if any one of the party breaks the covenant his body would suffer the same death as the animal suffered. There are two types of covenants recorded in the Bible and they are:

1. Conditional and
2. Unconditional

The covenant that God made with Abraham was Unconditional. The LORD said to Abram to take an heifer of three years old, a she goat of three years old, a ram of three years old, turtle dove and a young pigeon and divide them in the midst and lay each piece one against another. Abram did as the LORD commanded him. He did not divide birds and when the fowls came down on the carcasses, he drove them away (Ref. Genesis 15:7-11)

As the dusk started growing a deep sleep fell upon Abram and lo, a horror of great darkness fell upon him. The LORD spoke to Abram in his sleep and said to be sure that His seed shall be stranger in the land that is not theirs and shall serve the nation which will afflict them for four hundred years and that the LORD will judge that nation.

As a seal affixed to the covenant by the LORD the burning lamp of the LORD passed between those pieces. It may be noted here that Abram did not pass between the divided pieces which clearly indicates that it was one sided agreement. In the same day the LORD made a covenant with Abram that He gave the land to him from the river of Egypt unto the great river, the river Euphrates; this land is commonly called as the "fertile crescent".

Obviously, as seen in the Scriptures the word of the LORD with regard to their bondage of slavery was fulfilled when the children of Israel served Pharaoh of Egypt for four hundred years and, thereafter, God judged Pharaoh and Egypt.

The covenant that was made between God and Moses was conditional, that is to say, if they did what the LORD said to them, then God would do what He promised to them. However, the covenant that the LORD made with Abram was one sided, that is, the LORD made the covenant with Abram and He will fulfill His covenant no matter what the seed of Abram would do. God's promise will never fail and He will not go back on anyone of His promises. The LORD's covenant with Abram was from the LORD and He did not put a condition to fulfill His promise. (Ref. Genesis Chapter 15)

The LORD said to Abram as we read in Genesis Chapter 17 that he shall circumcise the flesh of his foreskin and it shall be a token of the covenant. He also said that every male of eight days old shall be circumcised among his people. Whoever did not obey this command of the LORD was cut off from the lineage of Abram but still the covenant the LORD made with Abram was not treated as abrogated.

The LORD's Promise still stands to be fulfilled in the lives of the descendants of Abraham. The LORD gave privilege to those who are bought with money by Abram and his descendants to reap the blessings of Abram when they are circumcised and otherwise they do not. (Ref. Genesis 17:11-14)

New Testament believer can be sure that it is not by keeping the Law of Moses that the promises are inherited but by the promise that the LORD made to Abraham (Cf. Galatians 4:7, Romans 8:17, Romans 10:17, Ephesians 2:8)

"For if the inheritance be of the law, it is no more of promise: but God gave it to Abraham by promise" (Galatians 3:18)

"For with the heart man believeth unto righteousness; and with the mouth confession is made unto salvation" (Romans 10:10)

# CHAPTER 5
# NO WEAPON SHALL PROSPER

"No weapon that is formed against thee shall prosper; and every tongue that shall rise against thee in judgment thou shalt condemn. This is the heritage of the servants of the LORD, and their righteousness is of me, saith the LORD". (Isaiah 54:17)

This verse basically points to the protection that God assures to the children of Israel but as the children of God through faith in him and saved by the blood of Jesus Christ every one of us who had the experience of salvation can claim it.

This is not a blanket promise to everyone but only to those Christians who truly serve Lord Jesus Christ. No weapon either in words, or with swords, or of arms of any kind will prosper against the Children of Israel and likewise no weapon formed against the children of God shall prosper.

Israel will be restored and God will surely take care of them. Pray for the peace of Jerusalem. God said whoever blesses Abraham will be blessed and whoever curses Abraham will be cursed. If we want truly blessings from God never ever curse Abraham or the children of Israel.

Isaiah Chapter 54 as a whole is addressed to the children of Israel, who have played harlot as far as their faithfulness and obedience to the Lord, is concerned. They have been asked time and again by God to be faithful to the living God, the God of Abraham, the God of Isaac, and the God of Jacob, yet they have gone to other gods and worshipped them.

Our God does not accept any one worshipping the idols and other gods. He will not share his glory with anybody else, leave alone giving away his glory; never does he give his glory to anybody. He is the God of gods. He has promised the land of Canaan, the land where milk and honey flow. This land is blessed and God promised to give to the children of Israel. They have never been able to conquer the whole Promised Land until now because they never recognized Messiah.

Most of them either believed that their Messiah has not yet come or they are atheists. God chastised them several times and in spite of facing such chastening from God, the children of Israel had been disobedient to God. They denied the Son of God as their Messiah and they have not yet realized that Lord Jesus Christ was the Messiah. They have been handed over to their enemies several times because of their disobedience. They had been taken captive by Assyrians and Babylonians and they are scattered.

Some of them have returned to Israel and there is a free Nation now, yet the return of Jews in full is not yet completed. They are yet to get hold of their Promised Land in full. Presently they are occupying only a part of the Promised Land.

In spite of all these, the children of Israel are God's people. God said just as hen gathers her children under her wings he will gather them under his wings. He will give them the Promised Land but not before they undergo the "great tribulation" also called "Jacob's Trouble" in the seventieth week of prophesy that is in Daniel 9th Chapter.

The married wife represents the children of Israel, the ancient Jewish Church, while the children of desolate represent the gentile Church, which took birth when Jews rejected Jesus as their Messiah.

In Isaiah Chapter 54:1 God asks the barren woman to break forth into singing because the children of Gentiles have been accepted into the Church and it is larger than the Jewish Church. The Church, which is the bride of Jesus, consists of Jews and Gentiles and it is above Israel.

"Sing, O barren, thou that didst not bear; break forth into singing, and cry aloud, thou that didst not travail with child: for more are the children of the desolate than the children of the married wife, saith the LORD". (Isaiah 54:1)

It was a mystery hidden in God and that mystery was revealed in Acts 13:46-47, Romans 11th Chapter and Ephesians Chapters 1 to 3 that salvation is made available to Gentiles.

"Then Paul and Barnabas waxed bold, and said, it was necessary that the word of God should first have been spoken to you: but seeing ye put it from you, and judge yourselves unworthy of everlasting life, lo, we turn to the Gentiles. For so hath the Lord commanded us, saying, I have set thee to be a light of the Gentiles, that thou shouldest be for salvation unto the ends of the earth". (Acts 13:46-47)

# CHAPTER 6
# THE LAND OF GOSHEN

In the land of Goshen there lived a great family. God chose the family and the land that they should live in their turbulent times. God gave Jacob and his children the land of Goshen in Egypt, when they came over from Canaan to have food during the great second famine. The first famine was during Abraham, ass recorded in Genesis 12:10.

Joseph was one among the twelve children of Jacob, whose grandfather was Abram. God changed his name as "Abraham" and his wife's as "Sarah". Abraham and Sarah were long dead when Jacob their grandson came into Egypt. There were very significant incidences in the lives of Abraham, Isaac, and Jacob. Isaac was the promised son, who was blessed.

To Abraham was born Ishmael by Hagar the handmaid of Sarai. Ishmael was born twelve years before Isaac was born, and yet God said in no less strong words that it was Isaac, the son of Abraham and Sarah, who would receive the blessings because he was the promised child.

In the land of Canaan, where Abraham, Isaac and Jacob lived in different periods of time, there occurred famine three times – one each during the periods if these patriarchs.

It was a marvelous deliverance for Sarai, wife of Abram, from the hands of Abimelech, king of Egypt, who could have had her, but for God's intervention. Abram forced Sarai to depart from telling the truth for the sake of protecting his own life. The truth was that Sarai was his wife, and before his marriage with her, she was his half-sister. After marriage she was not his half-sister, but his wife. However, Abram forced her in the land of Egypt to say that she was his sister.

Sarai was no doubt his half-sister but not after he married her. Sarai was his wife, and yet, he for the sake of not getting killed for her sake, handed over his wife to the lies, thus stumbling in his faith.

It was very unpleasing act before God that Abram, who was a man of faith, and to whom his faith was reckoned as righteousness, stumbled in his faith, first by travelling to Egypt, and second by fearing that he would be killed for his extremely beautiful Sarai sake. Abimelech, king of Egypt desired to have her. However, although Abimelech took Sarai in to his house, yet he could not lay his hand on her because God was with her.

God protected Sarai. The LORD interfered strongly by inflicting Abimelech and his family with plagues for Sarai. Abimelech sensed the strong outstretched hand of God and sought the truth from Abram as to who Sarai was. When Abram revealed the truth that Sarai was his wife, and he told a lie for fear, Abimelech admonished him and said to him to take his wife and go away.

Man is feeble and frail and no one is perfect. God, who is longsuffering, and ever present to help His children, protected and delivered Sarai. She was chosen by God to become the mother of the children of Israel.

Next, when there was a second famine during the period when Isaac was in Canaan, he and his family migrated to Gerar in the land of Philistines, where Abimelech was the king. (Abimelech during the period of Isaac was another king and not the one who was king during the period of Abram). God said to Isaac not to go to Egypt, and he obeyed God. Yet he sinned in a similar way his father did, by calling his wife as his sister. King Abimelech saw Isaac sporting his wife Rebecca, and called for him. When the king sought the truth, Isaac confessed that he feared his life that someone may kill him for Rebecca, who was also an extremely beautiful lady, and, therefore, he said to her to say that she was Isaac's sister. Abimelech was angry at Isaac and said to him to take his wife and go away. He also said to all the people that none should touch Rebecca. Thus Isaac was admonished by pagan king. This is how God protected Rebecca.

The third famine was in Canaan during the period when Joseph was the second in authority in Egypt, where Pharaoh was the king.

When Joseph broke out in tears before his brothers saying he was their brother, he gave glory to God and said he was sent to the land of Egypt beforehand to save the children of Jacob, who was renamed as "Israel" by God.

Jacob and his family were Hebrews they were all shepherds by profession. Joseph's brothers were all shepherds. Egyptians hated Hebrews. Joseph was Governor in the land of Egypt, and he being the second in command in the land of Egypt had much influence with Pharaoh, who readily conceded the request of Joseph and allowed Joseph's entire family to live in the land of Goshen during the famine.

Pharaoh identified the land of Goshen as the best of all the lands. Goshen was a land where Egyptians' cattle grazed and the land was called the "land of Goshen". It was a pastoral district. The LORD chose the land for them and He blessed it.

Although the children of Israel were happy when Pharaoh was on the throne and Joseph was Governor in the land, yet there arose a king in Egypt who did not know who Joseph was. He subjected them to harsh labor, even to the extent of not providing raw material for making bricks. The king feared that the children of Israel would be large in number and they would become a threat for him to face.

The children of Israel worked as slaves in Egypt for four hundred years and cried to the Lord to redeem them from the bondage of slavery. God heard their cry and provided them a leader who would redeem them from their slavery.

It was Moses, who was chosen by God to be their leader.

# CHAPTER 7
# THE LORD ANSWERS PRAYERS

And the LORD said, I have surely seen the affliction of my people which are in Egypt, and have heard their cry by reason of their taskmasters; for I know their sorrows; (Exodus 3:7)

The children of Israel served as slaves in Egypt for four hundred and when they cried to God He heard them, knew their sorrows and helped them out from their taskmasters. The LORD delivered the children of Israel with His mighty hand and outstretched arm from the bondage of slavery under Pharaoh and led them through wilderness from Egypt out unto Canaan.

When the plagues came upon the land of Egypt at the behest of the LORD, He safeguarded the children of Israel in the land of Goshen. They were neither affected by those pestilences nor were their cattle suffered diseases. God spared the first born children of all the Israelites by passing over their homes on seeing the blood on the door posts, but killed every first born of Egyptians including that of Pharaoh.

Pharaoh, his army and chariots were drowned in the Red sea. God turned bitter water into sweet water at 'Marah" for the sake of Israelites when they murmured for water. God provided heavenly food, the 'manna' for them every day and quails every evening. The manna tasted like coriander and like wafers dipped in honey and quails were meat food for them, yet they murmured against God. The angel of the LORD stood as pillar of fire behind them while they walked slowly on the dry land in the midst of the Red Sea. God protected them from Pharaoh who moved fast with his army in his chariots to capture the children of Israel.

In spite of God delivering them from the bondage of slavery and leading them to the Promised Land the children of Israel murmured throughout their journey which resulted in their wandering in the wilderness for forty years and none but Joshua, the son of Nun, and Caleb, the son of Jephunneh, of the generation that left Egypt reached Canaan, the land that flowed with milk and honey. Even Moses, their leader did not enter Canaan, because He violated God's command at one point of time.

Man in his best state is vanity simply for the reason that he is made of dust of the ground. Because of the sin of Adam and Eve man has to live by hard work until he returns to the ground. Man is dust and he will return to dust. (Genesis 2:7, Genesis 3:19) It is God's grace that we are saved from perishing eternally. As psalmist says God knows our frame and remembers that we are made of dust. (Psalm 103:14). He hears us when we cry to Him and answers our prayers. He gives salvation to those who call upon Him.

Later in due course of time after King Solomon, the 'House of Israel' was carried away captive by Assyrians who spoke a different tongue that they did not understand.

He taught them precept upon precept, line upon line, here a little and there a little just as father and mother would teach their child the alphabets of a language, and yet they disobeyed God and worshipped idols resulting in Assyrians talking to them different tongue that they did not understand and Assyrians taking them captive (Isaiah 28:10-13).

God told the children of Israel to make record of how he provided them food in the wilderness after leaving Egypt. God told them to store an "Omer" full with the 'manna' to show to their children in the subsequent generations as a sign for them proclaiming the wonderful way God provided them food.

Jesus died for our sake bearing our sin upon him. He was buried and rose from the dead on the third day and ascended into heaven and seated on the right hand of the Majesty. He will come back soon! Believe in Jesus and remember His death, burial and in his resurrection, and ascension. As a father sitting with his arms spread to receive his lost child God is waiting for Israelites to accept Jesus as their Messiah.

Seek ye the LORD while he may be found, call ye upon him while he is near: (Isaiah 55:6)

# CHAPTER 8
# THE PLAGUES IN EGYPT

## THE THREE SIGNS

And Moses answered and said, but, behold, they will not believe me, nor hearken unto my voice: for they will say, The LORD hath not appeared unto thee.

1. And the LORD said unto him, what is that in thine hand? And he said, a rod. And he said, Cast it on the ground. And he cast it on the ground, and it became a serpent; and Moses fled from before it.

2. And the LORD said unto Moses, Put forth thine hand, and take it by the tail. And he put forth his hand, and caught it, and it became a rod in his hand: That they may believe that the LORD God of their fathers, the God of Abraham, the God of Isaac, and the God of Jacob, hath appeared unto thee. And the LORD said furthermore unto him, Put now thine hand into thy bosom. And he put his hand into his bosom: and when he took it out, behold, his hand was leprous as snow. And he said, put thine hand into thy bosom again. And he put his hand into his bosom again; and plucked it out of his bosom, and, behold, it was turned again as his other flesh. And it shall come to pass, if they will not believe thee, neither hearken to the voice of the first sign, that they will believe the voice of the latter sign.

3. And it shall come to pass, if they will not believe also these two signs, neither hearken unto thy voice, that thou shalt take of the water of the river, nor pour it upon the dry land: and the water which thou takes out

of the river shall become blood upon the dry land. (Exodus 4:1-9)

## ONLY ONE SIGN WAS SHOWN

And the LORD spake unto Moses and unto Aaron, saying, When Pharaoh shall speak unto you, saying, Shew a miracle for you: then thou shalt say unto Aaron, Take thy rod, and cast it before Pharaoh, and it shall become a serpent. And Moses and Aaron went in unto Pharaoh, and they did so as the LORD had commanded: and Aaron cast down his rod before Pharaoh, and before his servants, and it became a serpent. Then Pharaoh also called the wise men and the sorcerers: now the magicians of Egypt, they also did in like manner with their enchantments. For they cast down every man his rod, and they became serpents: but Aaron's rod swallowed up their rods. And he hardened Pharaoh's heart that he hearkened not unto them; as the LORD had said. (Exodus 7:8-13)

## PLAGUE - DEFINITION

A "stroke" of affliction, or disease. Sent as a divine chastisement (Nu 11:33; 14:37; 16:46-49; 2Sa 24:21). Painful afflictions or diseases, (Le 13:3, 5, 30; 1Ki 8:37), or severe calamity (Mr. 5:29; Lu 7:21), or the judgment of God, so called (Ex 9:14). Plagues of Egypt were ten in number.

# CHAPER 9
# THE PLAGUES

## PLAGUE 1: RIVER NILE TURNED INTO BLOOD

The river Nile was turned into blood, and the fish died, and the river stank, so that the Egyptians loathed to drink of the river (Ex 7:14-25).

## PLAGUE 2: THE PLAGUE OF FROGS

The plague of frogs (Ex 8:1-15).

## PLAUGE 3: THE PLAGUE OF LICE

The plague of lice (Heb. kinnim, properly gnats or mosquitoes; comp. Ps 78:45; 105:31), "out of the dust of the land" (Ex 8:16-19).

## PLAUGE 4: THE PLAGUE OF FLIES

The plague of flies (Heb. arob, rendered by the LXX. dog-fly), Ex 8:21-24.

## PLAUGE 5: THE PLAGUE O F MURRAIN

The plague murrain (Ex 9:1-7) or epidemic pestilence. It carried off vast numbers of cattle in the field. Warning was given of its coming.

## PLAGUE 6: THE PLAGUE OF BOILS AND BLAINS

The sixth plague, of "boils and blains," like the third, was sent without warning (Ex 9:8-12). It is called (De 28:27) "the botch of Egypt," A.V.; but in R.V., "the boil of Egypt." "The magicians could not stand before Moses" because of it.

## PLAUGE 7: THE PLAGUE OF HAIL

The plague of hail, with fire and thunder (Ex 9:13-33). Warning was given of its coming. (Comp. Ps 18:13; 105:32-33).

## PLAGUE 8: THE PLAGUE OF LOCUSTS

The plague of locusts, which covered the whole face of the earth, so that the land was darkened with them (Ex 10:12-15). The Hebrew name of this insect, arbeh, points to the "multitudinous" character of this visitation. Warning was given before this plague came.

## PLAUGE 9: THE PLAGUE OF DARKNESS

After a short interval the plague of darkness succeeded that of the locusts; and it came without any special warning (Ex 10:21-29). The darkness covered "all the land of Egypt" to such an extent that "they saw not one another." It did not, however, extend to the land of Goshen.

## PLAGUE 10: THE FIRSTBORN KILLED

The last and most fearful of these plagues was the death of the first-born of man and of beast (Ex 11:4-5; 12:29-30). The exact time of the visitation was announced, "about midnight", which would add to the horror of the infliction. Its extent also is specified, from the first-born of the king to the first-born of the humblest slave, and all the first-born of beasts. But from this plague the Hebrews were completely exempted. The Lord "put a difference" between them and the Egyptians. (See Passover.)

"And the LORD said unto Moses, Wherefore criest thou unto me? Speak unto the children of Israel that they go forward: But lift thou up thy rod, and stretch out thine hand over the sea, and divide it: and the children of Israel shall go on dry ground through the midst of the sea". (Exodus 14:15-16)

One of the greatest miracles God has ever performed was to part the Red Sea to deliver his children of Israel from the bondage of Slavery and to drown the enemy forces of Pharaoh in the Red Sea.

After letting the children of Israel go out from Egypt to help them worship their God far away from the place of Egyptian gods, Pharaoh could not sit idle but to harbor the evil thoughts of Satan, once again, and pursued the children of God from behind chasing the children of Israel to capture them again and bring them back as slaves.

The children of Israel saw before them the Red Sea and behind them they saw the mighty forces of Pharaoh following them in the chariots. While the children of Israel, their children, and their cattle moved slowly they saw the chariots of Pharaoh speeding toward them to capture them. The children of God were filled with fear and cried out for help.

"And when Pharaoh drew nigh, the children of Israel lifted up their eyes, and, behold, the Egyptians marched after them; and they were sore afraid: and the children of Israel cried out unto the LORD" (Exodus 14:10)

Moses, their leader, cried unto God for help, and God provided them help on time. The Red Sea parted when Moses lifted up the rod over the Sea as directed by God. All the children of Israel moved out from the scene of danger to a place of safety beyond the sea. Pharaoh's speeding chariots could not catch the slow moving children of God, but instead they were drowned by God in the Red Sea; they along with their chariots.

While the children of God moved on the dry land in the midst of the Red Sea the Pharaoh's chariots and his army was drowned in the Red Sea.

In Exodus Chapter 13:17-18 we read that God deliberately did not take Israelites through a nearer way from Egypt to Canaan, which involves passing through the land of Philistines, but he took them through the wilderness of the Red Sea, inasmuch as God knew the weak hearts of Israelites, who would grumble against God for having led through the land of Philistines, where they had to face war. At the end of the chapter 13 we read that the LORD went before them by day in a pillar of cloud, and in the night in a pillar of fire to give them light. Thus they had the light the entire time they traveled in the wilderness. Holy and gracious God, the God of Israel, did not leave the children of Israel in darkness when they were passing through the wilderness but provided them light the entire time they traveled. God desired that their faith in Him should be strengthened.

Once when Jesus went walking on water towards the boat in which Peter and other disciples were sailing Peter desired that he may be allowed to walk on water. Jesus asked to walk on water and come near him but when Peter saw wind boisterous he was afraid and began to sink. He cried out to Lord Jesus to save him, and He saved him. Peter's little faith resulted in sinking but when he cried out to the Lord Jesus He saved Peter instantly (Matthew 14:28-31).

# GOD COULD HAVE STARTED IT ALL OVER AGAIN

"The Lord said to Moses, "How long will these people treat me with contempt? How long will they refuse to believe in me, in spite of all the signs I have performed among them? I will strike them down with a plague and destroy them, but I will make you into a nation greater and stronger than they." Numbers 14:11-12

Man's wickedness invited punishment when God brought huge deluge for forty days and forty nights during Noah's period, saving only Noah and his family and select creatures; and destruction of cities of Sodom and Gomorrah with fire and brimstone , saving only Lot.

But for the unconditional covenant the LORD made with Abraham, the children of Israel as a whole would have been destroyed for their repeated rebellion against the LORD. Each time He said He would not have any mercy on them Abrahamic covenant came into influence His decision and, therefore, chastised them and left them alone.

This reminds as to how God was angry with the children of Israel. God said He will not have mercy on them and He will not be their God, and yet when He remembers Abraham, He shows His undying love and mercy towards them. He calls them "Ammi" forgetting their rebellion.

"And she conceived again, and bare a daughter. And God said unto him, call her name Loruhamah: for I will no more have mercy upon the house of Israel; but I will utterly take them away. But I will have mercy upon the house of Judah, and will save them by the LORD their God, and will not save them by bow, nor by sword, nor by battle, by horses, nor by horsemen. Now when she had weaned Loruhamah, she conceived, and bare a son. Then said God, Call his name Loammi: for ye are not my people, and I will not be your God". (Hosea 1:6-9)

"Say ye unto your brethren, Ammi; and to your sisters, Ruhamah" (Hosea 2:1)

Exodus Chapters 14, 15, 16, 17 and Numbers 11-20 list their repeated rebellions and the LORD's chastisement. God did not leave His servant Moses also from being chastised. Moses was a descendant of Abraham, and of the promised seed Isaac. Going by the strong words God used in Exodus 32:10 and Numbers 14:12 it is evident that the LORD would not have hesitated to start all over again, and would have focused only on the descendants of Moses alone as a nation for Him.

"Now leave me alone so that my anger may burn against them and that I may destroy them. Then I will make you into a great nation." – Exodus 32:10

Interestingly, the LORD in His anger says, "How long these people treat me with contempt?" and still has compassion for them. The word "contempt" is a very strong word that meant they showed utter disrespect and indifference towards the LORD.

God could have simply wiped out the generations from Jacob, and focused only on the descendants of Moses; but alas! Ultimately Moses himself complained against the LORD and disobeyed God's command, showing how frail and feeble man at his best is.

"I will strike them down with a plague and destroy them, but I will make you into a nation greater and stronger than they." – Numbers 14:12

However, Moses intercedes for the people of Israel and reminds God that if He destroyed the children of Israel, people who hear about it would mock that the LORD slaughtered His own people (cf. Numbers 14:13-22).

The power of the children of God lies in reminding God His promises, His loving nature and reputation among nations in order to reclaim our blessings in the LORD. Jesus promised everlasting life to all those who believe in Him, and He will not go back on His promise. That is the reason why Jesus Christ, who is the Lord and builder of the house, is considered as greater than Moses who was faithful servant in the LORD's house (cf. Hebrews 1:1-14)

# CHAPTER 11
# OUR BLESSINGS IN ABRAHAM

Terah's sons were Abram, whose name was changed by God as "Abraham", and other two sons were Nahor and Haran.

Israel came into existence from the seed of Abraham. After Jacob was named as Israel as a consequence of blessings he received his posterity was called "Israel" and all others were called "Gentiles". Many years later after Solomon's death Israel was divided into two regions.

One was the "House of Israel" ruled by Jeroboam and other was "the House of Judah" ruled by Rehoboam. Much of what we read in the Bible, especially in the Old Testament, is all about God's dealing with Israel, the division of Israel into two, and God's promise to unite them.

God did not leave Gentiles aside. In due course of time God made Gentiles partakers of the Natural Olive Tree, the description of which can read in Jeremiah Chapter 11:16-17, Romans Chapters 9-11, Ephesians Chapter 3 and Galatians Chapter 3

Lot was the son of Haran who died in the land of Ur of Chaldees, before Terah died. Abram and Nahor took them wives. Abram's wife was Sarai and Nahor's wife was Milcah, who was the daughter of Haran. Terah went from Ur of Chaldees into the land of Canaan. He took with him Abram, his son, and Lot, the son of Haran, and Sarai, his 'daughter-in-law (Genesis 11:27-32). Abraham's son was Isaac and Isaac's son was Jacob. Jacob and his descendants are called "Israel". Chaldees was a region where heathen lived.

## ABRAHAM OBEYED

God said to Abram to leave the country, his relatives, his father's house and go to a land that He promised to give. God promised Abram that He will make Abram a great nation, bless him, and make his name great and that Abram will be a blessing to others. God said that whoever blesses Abram will be blessed and whoever curses Abram will be cursed. It was a great blessing that was given to Abraham. God said to Abraham "in thee shall all families of the earth be blessed". This is a very important blessing that should be taken note of. Abram believed and left his country along with his cousin's son, Lot and went to Canaan. While they were passing from Siechem to the plain of Moreh, God visited them and said that that land will be given to his posterity. Abram built an altar there for God. In the course of time as there was severe famine Abram went down to Egypt (Genesis 12:1-10). After having a bad experience in Egypt with the Pharaoh, who was punished by God, Abram moved with his wife and also Lot out of Egypt into the south.

"So Abram departed, as the LORD had spoken unto him; and Lot went with him: and Abram was seventy and five years old when he departed out of Haran". (Genesis 12:4)

Abram was very rich in cattle, in silver and gold. He moved further down to the place where he built an altar earlier and called on the name of the Lord. (Genesis 13:1-4)

## ABRAHAM'S FAITH

It indeed demands great deal of faith and courage to trust in God. Abraham believed God without raising any doubt. God promised Abraham blessings. Abraham moved from place to place honoring God. Abram obeyed God and did everything just as God told him to do. In all these Abram believed God without any doubt and it was counted to him as righteousness. Abram did not need to do anything other than trusting in God and go ahead in the paths ordered by God, and he obeyed God with faith. God honored his faith.

The faith Abram had on God, his obedience and honoring God need to be taken note of to see if we have such unflinching faith in God and obey him honoring him. In the New Testament as Apostle Paul and Stephen relate to the faith of Abram, who was later called "Abraham" by God, we clearly see the blessing of Abraham that we are bestowed with. God said to Abram that in him all nations will be blessed. This blessing was given to him before the Mosaic Law came into existence. Moses came many years later, and had the blessings and covenants from God of Israel. What is interesting is that even before Israel was blessed with blessings and covenants Abram was blessed and in him all nations were blessed. It was Abraham's unflinching faith that fetched him the honor of being reckoned as righteous. It is that kind of faith God expects us to have that we may be counted as righteous. In addition, those who believe in Jesus are made partakers of blessings and covenants of Jews (Ephesians Ch. 3:6).

## THE BLESSING OF ABRAHAM

When we consider this we stand in awe of God and glorify His name for blessing us with spiritual blessing inherited from Abraham. It is the promise of the Father that at the very moment we repent Holy Spirit indwells us. Jesus said that after ascending into heaven he would send the Promise of the Father and as promised the Holy Spirit came into this world to be our Comforter.

"And, behold, I send the promise of my Father upon you: but tarry ye in the city of Jerusalem, until ye be endued with power from on high". (Luke 24:49)

This giving of the Promise of the Father was fulfilled when his disciples were waiting at Jerusalem according to the instructions Lord Jesus gave them.

And they were all filled with the Holy Ghost, and began to speak with other tongues, as the Spirit gave them utterance. (Acts 2:4)

There is no more waiting needed for receiving the Holy Spirit because He is already there among us. The moment a person repents Holy Spirit indwells him or her. Apostle Paul writes in Galatians 3:7 that those which are of faith are the children of Abraham. This was an excellent gospel preached to Abraham way before he moved from the land of heathen to Canaan. The blessing that in Abraham (the then Abram) shall all the nations will be blessed and God will justify the heathen through faith was revealed by God to Abram.

Addressing the men of Israel Peter said that the God of Abraham, and of Isaac, and of Jacob glorified his Son Jesus, who was delivered up and the men of Israel denied Jesus as their Messiah in the presence of Pilate. Jesus was the Holy One, Just and Prince of life, who was crucified by them, but was raised from the dead by God. Peter and other disciples are witnesses to this. Peter also referred Abraham in his speech. (Acts 3:25)

Apostle Paul wrote about Abraham in Galatians 3:8

# CHAPTER 12
# SARAH RESCUED

We see in the following exposition that Abram, whose name God changed as "Abraham" feared and attempted to escape from trouble. Before we go into meditating on this thought let us recollect a verse from New Testament.

2 Timothy 3:16 reads...

"All scripture is given by inspiration of God, and is profitable for doctrine, for reproof, for correction, for instruction in righteousness..."

Now, here is the message from Genesis Chapter 20

After living for twenty years in Mamre Abram sojourned to Gerar. Abram was also called sojourner. He moved from one place to another. We are also sojourners on this earth looking forward to reaching heaven, which is our final destination.

When Abram moved from Mamre to Gerar, he was afraid for some time and tried to lie. That appears to us as unbecoming of his stature as the father of faith. It also renders him the character of cowardice. At a time when Sarai, whose name God changed later as "Sarah", was with a child, a promised seed in her womb, he asked her to say that she was his sister. He was worried more about his own life than living up to the truth.

Abram's own words say: "And yet indeed she is my sister; she is the daughter of my father, but not the daughter of my mother; and she became my wife. (Genesis 20:12)"

Yet, since he married her she was his wife. In his attempt to escape from trouble he said to her that she may tell Abimelech that she was his sister. Because of the fear Abram had Abimelech, the king of Gerar excels in character. The one who was about to commit sin is restored. Abimelech sent for Sarai, and took her to his house with a sinful desire to the take her to his bed. Note that usually one sin paves the way for another. It is indeed disastrous, especially when the sin of God's child paves the way for ungodly to commit sin. Let us, as the children of God, examine ourselves, if our ways are leading others to commit sins.

Because God made covenant with Abram He intervened and prevented the ugliest situation to come up. Psalmist asserts in Psalm 105:13-15 "When they went from one nation to another, from one kingdom to another people; He suffered no man to do them wrong: yea, he reproved kings for their sakes; saying, touch not mine anointed, and do my prophets no harm.

"And the LORD plagued Pharaoh and his house with great plagues because of Sarai Abram's wife" (Genesis 12:17)

God appeared to Abimelech, King of Gerar, in a dream and gave him warning that he was going to commit sin. God revealed to Abimelech that Sarai was Abram's wife. He also gets warning that if he forces her into illegal relationship he will face death. Abimelech pleads innocent before God and implores for mercy. He prays that he and his nation may not be punished. God grants Abimelech his petition and imputes him no sin.

One aspect that needs to be noted here is that a great deal of sin was devised but it was not executed. More often than not, God restrains people to commit sin.

No temptation is beyond the control of men, and in fact in every situation God provides a way out. It is by our willful act that we fall in to sin, or lead others into sin. In situations where we choose to fall willfully into sin against the will of God we are responsible and accountable. Let us be careful.

"There hath no temptation taken you but such as is common to man: but God is faithful, who will not suffer you to be tempted above that ye are able; but will with the temptation also make a way to escape, that ye may be able to bear it" (1 Corinthians 10:13)

# CHAPTER 13
# REBEKAH RESCUED

As the saying goes "Like father Like son", Isaac made the same mistake or call it 'sin' of forcing her to call herself as his sister in the land of Philistines. During the first famine as recorded in Genesis 12, Abram sojourned from Canaan to Egypt and forced his wife, Sarai to identify herself as his sister. It was by God's help that escaped sin when the LORD inflicted King Abimelech and his people with plagues that the king let her go without touching her.

Here, a similar incident happened. There was a second famine in the land of Canaan, and Isaac sojourned from Canaan to Philistine, where another king by the same title viz. Abimelech let Rebekah, the wife of Isaac, go free without touching her. The king saw Isaac sporting his wife Rebekah and questioned him as to why he lied to him saying she was his wife. Just as Abram said that he feared for his life, so did Isaac too saying he feared for his life. Go saved both the women from disastrous consequences (cf. (Genesis 26:1-11)

# CHAPTER 14
# ABRAHAM SEEKS ANSWERS

And Abraham drew near, and said, Wilt thou also destroy the righteous with the wicked? Peradventure there be fifty righteous within the city: wilt thou also destroy and not spare the place for the fifty righteous that are therein? That be far from thee to do after this manner, to slay the righteous with the wicked: and that the righteous should be as the wicked that be far from thee: Shall not the Judge of all the earth do right? And the LORD said, if I find in Sodom fifty righteous within the city, then I will spare all the place for their sakes. And Abraham answered and said, Behold now, I have taken upon me to speak unto the Lord, which am but dust and ashes: Peradventure there shall lack five of the fifty righteous: wilt thou destroy all the city for lack of five? And he said, if I find there forty and five, I will not destroy it. And he spake unto him yet again, and said, Peradventure there shall be forty found there. And he said, I will not do it for forty's sake. And he said unto him, Oh let not the Lord be angry, and I will speak: Peradventure there shall thirty be found there. And he said, I will not do it, if I find thirty there. And he said, Behold now, I have taken upon me to speak unto the Lord: Peradventure there shall be twenty found there. And he said, I will not destroy it for twenty's sake. And he said, Oh let not the Lord be angry, and I will speak yet but this once: Peradventure ten shall be found there. And he said, I will not destroy it for ten's sake. And the LORD went his way, as soon as he had left communing with Abraham: and Abraham returned unto his place. (Genesis 18:23-33)

# CHAPTER 15
# TRIUMPHANT HEZEKIAH

*"Be strong and courageous, be not afraid nor dismayed by the king of Assyria, nor by all the multitude that is with him: for there are more with us than with him" (2 Chronicles 32:7)*

God's name is greatly glorified by the victory the LORD gave King Hezekiah of Judah over King Sennacherib of Assyria. The LORD helps, protects and rescues them that depend on him, from serious situations.

Out of twenty kings of the southern kingdom of Israel, which was also called "Kingdom of Judah", there were only four who did that which was pleasing to the God. One of them was King Hezekiah. Other three were King Asa, King Jehoshaphat and King Josiah.

In contrast, there was not even a single king, among the nineteen kings, in the northern kingdom of Israel, who did not do that which was evil in the sight of the LORD. The kings of the Northern Kingdom of Israel, which was also known as the "House of Israel" consisting of the Ten Tribes of Israel, from King Jeroboam unto King Hoshea, who was the nineteenth and the last one, every one of them did that which was evil in the sight of the LORD.

None before King Hezekiah in the kingdom of Judah revered the LORD so much as he did. Young as he was at the age of 25 he became king over "Judah" and he reigned over the Kingdom of Judah for twenty nine years. As his devotion to the LORD was greatly pleasing to the LORD, He was with Hezekiah and the king prospered.

A close perusal as to why God was so pleased with Hezekiah reveals that he did put into practice the Commandments of God, especially the first two of the commandments which are...

*"Thou shalt have no other gods before me" Exodus 20:3*

*"Thou shalt not make unto thee any graven image, or any likeness of anything that is in heaven above, or that is in the earth beneath, or that is in the water under the earth" Exodus 20:4*

During the course of his reign King Hezekiah utterly destroyed the images of other gods into pieces, cut down groves and threw down the high places and altars out of all the provinces of Judah, Benjamin, Ephraim and Manasseh.

He appointed priests and Levites to offer burnt offerings and peace offerings. He also set apart his portion of the substance for burnt offerings and peace offerings every morning and every evening, and burnt offerings for the Sabbaths, and for the new moons and for the set feasts as written in the law of the LORD (cf. 2 Chronicles 31:1-9, Leviticus 23:1-43).

He commanded the people that they give their portion of the priests and the Levities. The children of Israel obeyed his commandments and offered in abundance their first-fruits of their produce and brought tithe of oxen and sheep and laid them in heaps. When Hezekiah saw the heaps of offerings he praised the LORD and blessed his people.

King Hezekiah not only removed the high places of worship and broke the images, cut down the groves, but he also broke into pieces the image in brass of the serpent that Moses had made. Hezekiah noticed that the brass serpent that was made by Moses, as a sign to life for those who disobeyed the LORD, had soon become an idol for worship. Instead of remembering God's provision of fresh life to them, they burnt incense to the image of brass serpent. Hezekiah was furious over their fallacy in belief, and destroyed the image of the brass serpent.

It may be recalled that the LORD God spoke to the children of Israel through Moses that there is a provision for covering of their sins. It was by the lifting of the brass serpent on a pole, and the sinner, who was bitten by the serpent looking at it. In doing so the sinner would live (cf. Numbers 21:7-9).

This sign was foreshadow of the substance that was fulfilled when Lord Jesus Christ, who was lifted on the cross to die on behalf us fulfilling the prophecies that whoever believed on Him would not perish but have everlasting life.

Lord Jesus quoted in His conversation with Nicodemus of this provision and pointed to His own future sacrificial death on behalf of sinners.

*"And as Moses lifted up the serpent in the wilderness, even so must the Son of man be lifted up: That whosoever believeth in him should not perish, but have eternal life" (John 3:14-15)*

Jesus, who was born a Jew, lived among his brethren Jews and spoke the words of the Father, and died for the sins of the whole world. He became sacrifice on behalf of us and, therefore, there is no other sacrifice needed. There is no salvation to anyone except believing in the efficacy of His precious blood.

Those who looked at the brass serpent in the wilderness lived. However, gradually the focus and the purpose of lifting of the brass serpent was lost when the children of Israel made the brass serpent an idol of worship.

Hezekiah realized their folly of worshipping the idol. Therefore, he broke the brazen serpent and called it "Nehustan", which means it was mere brass-piece (cf. 2 Kings 18:4).

Hezekiah rebelled against King of Assyria and did not serve him. The LORD was with him, and, therefore, he defeated Philistines and Assyrians and prospered wherever he went forth. (Cf.2 Kings 18:8 and 19:35-37).

As for the fall of northern kingdom of Israel the LORD permitted it because of their disobedience to the LORD (cf. 2 Kings 18:9-12).

In Hezekiah's fourth year of reign Shalmanezer, king of Assyria, attacked Samaria, besieged it and took full control of it in two years. He took Israel captive and moved them to Halah, Habor and to the cities of Medes. The LORD gave them over to King of Assyria because they transgressed God's covenant and were disobedient to the Laws given by God through His servant Moses.

In the fourteenth year of King Hezekiah, a pagan king whose name was Sennacherib from Assyria sent letters to Hezekiah. Sennacherib was boastful, pride and blasphemous. He ridiculed the God of Hezekiah and sent letters to the latter with a crooked desire to score a victory over "kingdom of Judah". He set his ambition, initially to besiege Lachish (vs.9), but heard that King Hezekiah was fortifying Jerusalem and encouraging his people to stand against the invasion.

Sennacherib, king of Assyria came up against Hezekiah in the fourteenth year of latter's reign and fenced cities of Judah and took them. Lachish was a very strategic city where the armies pitch one against another for war and it is at that city that Sennacherib came and boasted in pride.

Hezekiah, king of Judah was disappointed and, therefore, sent word to Sennacherib that he would pay penalty for not serving him. Sennacherib imposed on Hezekiah a fine of three hundred talents of silver and thirty talents of gold, which was huge sum. Hezekiah raised the sum from the house of the Lord, treasures of the king's house and even from the gold from the doors of the Solomon's temple and gave to it king Sennacherib.

It is disheartening to note that the King, who had so much faith in God, and who did right in the sight of the LORD, and trusted in LORD's help more than anyone else's in the Kingdom of Judah, got disappointed when he was faced with some trying situation such as Sennacherib taking over Lachish and cities of Judah. Indeed, he showed that he was also fallible and human just as any one of us. However, God was compassionate to him when he prayed to Him.

It is worth quoting Prophet Elijah's experience. Elijah, who was so courageous a prophet, feared Jezebel and ran from her presence to hide. However, he soon recovered from that fear when the angel of the LORD comforted him. He heard the voice of the LORD not in strong wind, or in the earthquake, or fire, but in a still small voice that said "What doest thou here, Elijah".

The prophet listened to the voice of the LORD the God of hosts, and spoke to him in a complaining tone that the children of Israel have forsaken the covenant of the LORD and threw down the altars and killed prophets with the sword. Continuing his speech he went on saying that he was the only one left who did everything right in the sight of the LORD. The LORD gave him one more assignment of anointing Hazael to be king over Syria and of anointing Jehu, the son of Nimshi to be king over Israel. God said to Elijah that He had seven thousand in Israel who have not bowed their knees to Baal (cf. 1 Kings 19:14-19).

Such stumbling may come in the way of the children of God but God does not leave them as orphans without help. He will protect and rescue them. Hezekiah yielded to the demands of Sennacherib but ultimately the victory belonged to Hezekiah.

Sennacherib demanded three hundred talents of silver and thirty talents of gold, which Hezekiah gave to him from the house of the LORD and from the treasures of his house. Sennacherib did not keep calm even after receiving that which he demanded, but sent threatening words through his emissaries.

Sennacherib sent Tartan, Rabsaris and Rabshakeh from Lachish to Hezekiah and they stood by the conduit of the upper poor and spoke to Eliakim and Shebna, and Joah of Hezekiah's representatives and insulted them and questioned them as to who would or which God could save them from his attack.

They went to Jerusalem and stood by the conduit of the upper pool, and called the king. Their leader Rabshakeh spoke to the representatives of Hezekiah. He not only spoke blasphemous speeches against the living God of Hezekiah but boasted of great victories of Sennacherib and in his acts of courage. He read the letters from Sennacherib with the hope of frightening Hezekiah and his people. His tactics were loathsome and were directed to terrify common people and to persuade them to desert Hezekiah. He demanded Hezekiah to surrender the city (cf. 2 Kings 18:13-20).

Rabshakeh cried with a loud voice in Jewish language saying Hezekiah's God cannot save the people of Judah and said to them to make agreement with king of Assyria but he people held peace at the command of Hezekiah. Rabshakeh told the king Hezekiah about the blasphemous words that Rabshakeh spoke at the instance of Sennacherib and it made Hezekiah a grievous man.

Sennacherib in his pride blasphemed the living God of Hezekiah, and compared the God of heavens, who is the maker of heaven and earth to that of idols of the nations. He upheld the work of men's hands greater than the works of living God and depicted his utmost contempt for the living God, the God of Abraham, the God of Isaac, and the God of Jacob.

Addressing Hezekiah's people he said:

*"Now therefore let not Hezekiah deceive you, nor persuade you in this way, neither yet believe him: for no god of any nation or kingdom was able to deliver his people out of my hand, and out of the hand of my fathers: how much less shall your God deliver you out of my hand?" (2 Chronicles 32:15)*

Sennacherib's rude and impertinent and intemperate behavior filled with profane attitude was the reason for his downfall and punishment. Before it is too long there came the downfall of Sennacherib, the proud king.

King Hezekiah rent his clothes, covered himself in sackcloth and went to the LORD for help. Isaiah heard about Hezekiah's concern and conveyed to him message that "Thus saith the

LORD, Be not afraid of the words which thou hast heard, with which the servants of the king of Assyria have blasphemed me".

Hezekiah prayed to the LORD saying "O LORD God of Israel, which dwellest between the cherubims, thou art the God, even thou alone, of all the kingdoms of the earth; thou hast made heaven and earth".

King Hezekiah recovered from fear and brought Sennacherib to his feet with the help of mighty God in whom he trusted. Sennacherib's blasphemous words, arrogant speech yielded him absolutely nothing. The Lord sent an angel who destroyed everyone in the Sennacherib's camp and saved Hezekiah and the inhabitants of Jerusalem from his hand.

The LORD answered Hezekiah's prayer and sent His angel, who went out and "smote in the camp of the Assyrians an hundred fourscore and five thousand: and when they arose early in the morning, behold, they were all dead corpses". (1 Kings 19:35)

"And for this cause Hezekiah the king, and the prophet Isaiah the son of Amoz, prayed and cried to heaven. And the LORD sent an angel, who cut off all the mighty men of valor, and the leaders and captains in the camp of the king of Assyria. So he returned with shame of face to his own land. And when he had come into the house of his god, sons that came forth of his own body struck him down there with the sword" (2 Chronicles 32:20-21).

The angel of the LORD went out in the night and killed hundred fourscore and five thousand men of Sennacherib's men and they were all dead corpses by morning. Sennacherib in shame left and returned to Nineveh where he worshipped in the house of Nisroch, his god only to face most ignominious death by the hands of his own two sons, Adrammelech and Sharezer (cf. 2 Kings 19:35-37 )

Thereafter many brought gifts unto the Lord to Jerusalem and gifts to Hezekiah, who was magnified in the sight of all the nations from then on. Those who take refuge in the Lord will find victory in him and respect in the sight of men.

"Thus the LORD saved Hezekiah and the inhabitants of Jerusalem from the hand of Sennacherib the king of Assyria, and from the hand of all others, and guided them on every side. And many brought gifts unto the LORD to Jerusalem, and precious gifts to Hezekiah king of Judah: so that he was magnified in the sight of all nations from that time on" (2 Chronicles 32:22-23).

## GOD BLESSED HEZEKIAH

Every believer in God is chastened by the LORD, at some point or other or even several times, either to bring him closer to God or to test his faith in order that he may become stronger in faith in God, or as a result of some sin committed by him. King Hezekiah was no exception.

Hezekiah showed his natural weakness just as any believer would stumble some times by yielding initially to Sennacherib and agreeing to pay the penalty levied by Sennacherib.

In the course of time when Hezekiah fell sick unto death, Isaiah went to him and said to him that unless he sets his house in order he would die and not live. The reason for him to receive admonition by the prophet Isaiah is known to God.

Instead of raising counter questions or disobeying the warning, Hezekiah readily yielded to God's warning through the prophet and turned his face to the wall and wept sore before the LORD. When Hezekiah wept sore and yielded to the warning from God, there was a pleasing reply from the LORD. Subsequent events show how the LORD gave him signs to know that He will be healed and fifteen years would be added to his life (cf. Isaiah 37:36-38:1; 2 Kings 20:1-6).

Hezekiah prayed to the LORD and the LORD blessed him by extending his life by fifteen years. Hezekiah reigned successfully for fifteen more years and he slept with his fathers and Manasseh reigned in his stead.

God is our rock of refuge and He helps us in all situations, whether they be small or trying situations when we seek His help.

"But the LORD is my defense; and my God is the rock of my refuge" (Psalms 94:22)

Through the life of Hezekiah we can be sure of God's help and protection of those who depend on God and live obeying His commands and statutes.

# CHAPTER 16
# DANIEL'S FOOD CHOICE

*And at the end of ten days their countenances appeared fairer and were fatter in flesh than all the youths that ate of the king's delicate food. (Daniel 1:15)*

Out of the total number of twenty kings ruled southern kingdom of Israel, Jehoiakim was the eighteenth one. He ruled the Southern Kingdom of Israel, which was also known as "House of Judah" for eleven years from 605 B.C to 598 BC.

In the third year of Jehoikim's rule, Babylonian King Nebuchadnezzar invaded the Jerusalem and besieged it. The LORD gave Jehoiakim and his kingdom into the hand of Nebuchadnezzar as a result of Israel's disobedience to keep the Sabbath for a total number of seventy times. They were supposed to keep Sabbath not only on every seventh day, but also every seventh year. Therefore, the LORD gave them over to their enemies, who took them captive for seventy years.

As for Northern Kingdom, which was also known as the "House of Israel" none of the total number of nineteen kings who ruled the "House of Israel" did good in the sight in the LORD. They all did evil in the sight of the LORD, and therefore, God scattered the entire "House of Israel" into the world. It is nearly impossible to trace them back as to where they are now.

Nebuchadnezzar, who took the "House of Judah" captive ordered part of the vessels of the House of God to be taken into the land of Shinar to be placed in the house of his god. He also said to Ashpenaz the master of eunuchs, to take away certain children of Israel, who were without any blemish, well favored, wise, and cunning in knowledge, who understood science, and had the ability to stand in king's palaces. They were to be from the seed of king Jehoiakim, and of the princes.

Those children who were qualified to be in the King's palace were Daniel, Hananiah, Mishael, and Azariah, whose names were changed by the King. They were named after his gods. Daniel was named as "Belteshazzar, Shadrach, Meshach, and Abednego respectively.

However, scriptures call Daniel by his original name, and the other three by the names that Nebuchadnezzar gave them. Besides Daniel the prophet, there were three others in the Bible that were called Daniel. Those names are found in 1 Chronicles 3:1, Ezra 8:2, and Nehemiah 10:6. These names should not be confused with Daniel the prophet's name.

Nebuchadnezzar ordered that the best food, which he was eating, should be given to Daniel, Shadrach, Meshach and Abednego. King's food consisted of meat and wine, and may also have been rich in other ingredients that had high proteins, carbohydrates, etc. Probably they may and may have been first offered to his gods before serving. However, Daniel purposed in his heart that he would not get defiled with the king's meat and wine and, therefore, preferred to eat vegetables and drink water.

He was very sure that the food that God gives him would be richer and healthier than the king's food.

God honors those who honor him. Daniel was educated and trained in the knowledge and the language of Chaldeans according to the desire of the king. The LORD brought Daniel into favor and tender love with the princes of the eunuchs.

*As for these four youths, God gave them knowledge and skill in all learning and wisdom; and Daniel had understanding in all visions and dreams. (Daniel 1:17)*

Daniel requested Ashpenaz the chief of his eunuchs that he may be spared from eating king's food and be given vegetables and water. Ashpenaz expressed his concern that Daniel may look weak and unhealthy when the time comes for him to stand before for a test before being chosen to stand in the king's palace to help the king.

*Prove thy servants, I beseech thee, ten days; and let them give us pulse to eat, and water to drink; (Daniel 1:12)*

However, Daniel insisted on having only ordinary food and was confident that God would help him to have excellent countenance before the king in all respects. He requested Ashpenaz to give him ten days to prove his belief. Ashpenaz reluctantly agreed and after the lapse of ten days Daniel, who refused to eat meat and drink wine, and ate vegetables and water, was brought before he king. Indeed, Daniel was seen ten times better than all the astrologers and magicians who were in the kingdom.

Daniel prospered in the kingdom of Babylon by the grace of God of heavens, whom He acknowledged as His God. Daniel never gave any importance to his own intelligence, or efficiency but gave all the importance and prominence to the LORD God of Israel for his success.

# CHAPTER 17
# NEBUCHADNEZZAR'S DREAM

Doesn't it appear strange that someone says that he saw a dream and demands interpretation of it after forgetting the dream? Nevertheless, king Nebuchadnezzar did the very thing which seems to us strange. Is there anything hard for the LORD? He knows our hearts and the thoughts that are in our minds. He searches men by their thoughts in their minds and knows the depth of their hearts.

If we recall the miracles done by Moses and Aaron before Pharaoh where the magicians also turned their staffs into serpents, but alas! The serpent that came alive from Aaron's staff swallowed the serpents that came alive from the rods of magicians (cf. Exo. 7:8-12).

Here was a life threatening situation for magicians, sorcerers, and Chaldeans under his command to interpret the dream of Nebuchadnezzar that he forgot. The king called them and said to them that his spirit was troubled, and he is robbed of his sleep.

The Chaldeans insisted the king in Aramaic language to tell the dream in order that they may interpret his dream and explain the meaning thereof to him; but the king repeatedly said to them that he forgot the dream. The king said it was a command from him to call for to remembrance the dream and explain the interpretation of the dream. The king a warning that if they do not let him know the dream and the interpretation thereof, he would cut the in pieces, and that their houses will be made dunghill. On the contrary, he said if they let him know the dream and the interpretation he would give them gifts and rewards and bestow upon them great honor.

The Chaldeans answered the king and said to him that, except for gods who have no flesh in them but only spirit, there is not a single person on the earth who could make the king known of his dream and tell him the interpretation of his dream.

Nebuchadnezzar was furious at this assertion by the Chaldeans whom he trusted and ordered destruction of all the wise men in his kingdom.

It may be recalled of Abraham's quest to know from God as to what number of righteous people would form the yardstick for the LORD to cause righteous to perish along with the wicked. Abraham put forth first a number which was 50, and then 45, and then 40, and then 30, and then 20, and then 10 and sought each time very politely from the LORD if he would allow that number of righteous people to perish wicked. The LORD was very pleasant in His conversation with Abraham and said to him that, if He found as many number of righteous as Abraham put forward, He would not allow righteous to be destroyed along with the wicked.

The king's decree was let known very quickly to all the inhabitants of Babylon. Interestingly, there were four righteous, namely, Daniel, Shadrach, Meshach and Abednego in Babylon. The LORD protected all the four from severe persecutions.

Daniel inquired from Arioch the chief of the king's bodyguard, who went out to kill the wise men of Babylon, the reason for so severe decree. Daniel went to the king and said if some time were to be given to him he would let the King know his dream and the interpretation thereof.

Before Daniel took any decision about revealing the king's dream, he went to his friends Hananiah, Mishael, and Azariah and said to them to seek mercies of the living God to reveal the secret of the dream, in order that they may not perish along with the rest of the magicians, sorcerers and Chaldeans.

God knows the secrets of the hearts. God revealed the secret of Nebuchadnezzar's dream to Daniel in his night vision. Daniel thanked the LORD and proclaimed the greatness of the God of heavens He gave all the preeminence to the LORD God of heavens and said wisdom and might belong to the LORD.

Daniel did not take pride in whatever knowledge he had but gave God the glory for revelation the LORD made to him about Nebuchadnezzar's dream and without losing much time Daniel acknowledged the greatness of God and said wisdom and might are the LORD's

It is the LORD who changes times and seasons, and it is the LORD who deposes kings and authorities and replaces them at His will and according to His desire. It is the LORD who reveals secretes to His children. It is He who knows what is hidden in the darkness, because He is light and the lights resides in Him

Daniel thanked God and praised Him saying He is the God of his fathers. It is the LORD who gave wisdom and might to him and He thanked God for revealing king's dream and the secret of his dream.

Daniel went to Arioch and said to him to make him stand before the king in order that he may let the king know his dream and explain the meaning of his dream. Arioch was quick enough to bring Daniel before Nebuchadnezzar and said to him that he found Daniel who could tell him his dream and its explanation.

The king inquired of Daniel if he could let him know the dream and its interpretation thereof. Daniel took this opportunity and said to him that the secret that none of wise men, or the magicians, or the scribes, or astrologers in his kingdom could tell, is revealed to him by God of heavens, who knows all the secretes of every man.

Daniel continued saying it is the LORD who will reveal the dream and the secret of the dream to the king through him, whom the LORD uses as instrument in the hands of the LORD for His glory.

Daniel said the king's dream was about the end days of him and his kingdom. He went on revealing the dream and the interpretation thereof.

Daniel said to Nebuchadnezzar that the king saw in his dream a great image that stood before him. The image was mighty and its brightness excellent and its appearance was terrible and quite peculiar unseen by anyone any time. He went on describing the image and its interpretation.

Daniel said, the head of the image was made of fine gold, its chest and arms were made of silver, its belly and thighs were made of brass, its legs were made of iron and feet were made partly of iron and partly of clay. He continues saying the king saw a stone was cut out and there was not seen any hand cutting it.

The stone smote feet of iron and clay portion of the image, and broke them to pieces. Then the iron, the clay, the brass, the silver, and the gold, that is from bottom to the top of the image was broken into pieces together. They all at once fell together and became like the chaff during the threshing floors.

NEBUCHADNEZZAR'S DREAM IMAGE[1]

The image and it's prophetical significance is not only applicable to Nebuchadnezzar's time period but also to the subsequent kingdoms until Lord Jesus Christ's coming into this world in first time in the form of a servant and in the likeness of man, and then the second time in His glory in the clouds to receive His Church. Thereafter the Lord will reign for one

[1] Artwork by Jaden John Dennis, 7-year-old Grandson of the author Leslie M. John

thousand years. His Kingdom overthrows all other kingdoms present until that time. He is the King of kings and Lord of lords. It is quite necessary to understand that the stone became mountain gradually. It was gradual; not instant. Lord Jesus Christ's Kingdom has already started increasing gradually and will surely become one great Kingdom, which shall not end.

*"And there are seven kings: five are fallen, and one is, and the other is not yet come; and when he cometh, he must continue a short space. And the beast that was, and is not, even he is the eighth, and is of the seven, and goeth into perdition. And the ten horns which thou sawest are ten kings, which have received no kingdom as yet; but receive power as kings one hour with the beast. These have one mind, and shall give their power and strength unto the beast. These shall make war with the Lamb, and the Lamb shall overcome them: for he is Lord of lords, and King of kings: and they that are with him are called, and chosen, and faithful". (Revelation 17:10-14)*

The Lord reigns forever and ever. The kingdoms that follow Nebuchadnezzar fall one by one but the end was not yet. The end of worldly kingdoms come to pass when Lord Jesus Christ wages war against all principalities, evil forces and establishes His peaceful regime.

Lord Jesus Christ's Kingdom as seen of a mountain that emerges from a stone cut without hands, is an everlasting Kingdom. The stone strikes the bottom of the image resulting in every kingdom vanishing once for all never to rise again. The kingdoms that followed Nebuchadnezzar's period accurately correspond to historical kingdoms of Medo-Persia, Greece and Rome.

*"The ungodly are not so: but are like the chaff which the wind driveth away. Therefore the ungodly shall not stand in the judgment, nor sinners in the congregation of the righteous" (Psalms 1:4-5)*

The portions of different metals and the clay of the image as seen by the king in his dream did not fall one by one but as whole structure 'together' from bottom to top and became like chaff. The wind blew and It carried away the whole structure that fell down; not to be seen again. The kingdom of God will destroy the kingdoms of this world in one stretch and not piece by piece (cf. 2 Thessalonians 1:7-10)

Does it contradict that the kingdoms fall 'together' as it is written in Daniel 2:35? No! The kingdoms, as seen historically fell, no doubt, in succession, but in the context it refers to identify of their condition rather than referring to the "time".

Quote: The literal meaning of the word (חד chad used and חדה chădâh) is, "one," or "first." Ezra 4:8, "wrote a letter;" Ezra 5:13, "in the first year of Cyrus;" Ezra 6:2, "a roll;" Daniel 2:9; "there is but one decree for you;" Daniel 3:19, "heat the furnace one seven times hotter," etc. United with the preposition (כ k) it means "as one," like the Hebrew כאחד ke'echâd) - Ecclesiastes 11:6; 2 Chronicles 5:13; Ezra 2:64; Ezra 3:9; Isaiah 65:25. Unquote --- William Barnes

*"And to you who are troubled rest with us, when the Lord Jesus shall be revealed from heaven with his mighty angels, In flaming fire taking vengeance on them that know not God, and that obey not the gospel of our Lord Jesus Christ: Who shall be punished with everlasting destruction from the presence of the Lord, and from the glory of his power; When he shall come to be glorified in his saints, and to be admired in all them that believe (because our*

*testimony among you was believed) in that day" (2 Thessalonians 1:7-10)*

The stone that struck down the whole image, (not by part by part but at one stretch), became a great mountain and filled the earth. Mountain in Scriptures is a symbolism of kingdom (cf. Dan 2:35; Rev 13:1; 17:9-11) This signifies that worldly powers may rise one after another but they all will be smashed down by one great power that becomes like a great mountain and rules the world. The great power shown here is nothing but the Lord Jesus Christ, the Son of God, who will rule the whole world for one thousand years, when there shall be indescribable peace.

Nebuchadnezzar was compared to the greatest power in the world and was on the top. It was followed by kingdoms one inferior in sequence to the other, and lastly a kingdom that would be so brittle and feeble that it would be like iron mixed with clay.

God of heavens gave the kingdom to Nebuchadnezzar making him king of kings, with power, strength, and glory. The LORD made him so powerful and mighty that children of men, the beasts of the fields, and the fowl of the heavens were all given into his hands and made ruler over them. He was compared with the head of gold of the great image, but God comes down on all the worldly kingdom so furiously that none exists when he cuts them all off. Every kingdom will tumble down to utter destruction at the hands of Lord Jesus Christ.

Nebuchadnezzar pondered on the dream that Daniel revealed to him and the interpretation he detailed to him and fell upon his face and paid respects to Daniel. Thereafter he commanded that the people should offer an oblation and burn incense to him. The king said to Daniel that his God, that is Jehovah, is greater than any other god, and LORD of kings, and who reveals secrets His people. Thereafter the king made Daniel a great man, and not only he gave great gifts, but he bestowed upon him great respect by making him chief of the governors to rule over the whole province of Babylon, and over all the wise men of Babylon. Daniel preferred to be at the king's court and therefore, said to the king to give Shadrach, Meshach, and Abednego the powers to manage the affairs of the province of Babylon. (cf. Daniel 2:46-49)

King Nebuchadnezzar had no idea who the real God was. He fell prostrate to Daniel and worshipped him when Daniel revealed his dream and make him known of the interpretation of his dream. The dream and the interpretation, which God of heavens revealed to Daniel, was so accurate that the king was astonished and thought Daniel was divine, probably one such as of his gods. His misunderstanding does not end there but he continues to worship idols, until the LORD makes him a beast for seven periods of time.

Here in Daniel Chapter 3 King Nebuchadnezzar is seen making a golden image of three score cubits in height and six cubits of breadth of his god.

Psalmist makes mockery of idols saying they are made of "...*silver and gold, the work of men's hands. They have mouths, but they speak not: eyes have they, but they see not: They have ears, but they hear not: noses have they, but they smell not: They have hands, but they handle not: feet have they, but they walk not: neither speak they through their throat. They that make them are like unto them; so is every one that trusteth in them*". (Psalms 115:4-8)

*"They lavish gold out of the bag, and weigh silver in the balance, and hire a goldsmith; and he maketh it a god: they fall down, yea, they worship. They bear him upon the shoulder, they carry him, and set him in his place, and he standeth; from his place shall he not remove: yea, one shall cry unto him, yet can he not answer, nor save him out of his trouble"* (Isaiah 46:6-7)

Nebuchadnezzar set up the idol that he made, in the plain of Dura, which was in the province of Babylon. He ordered high officials in his kingdom to witness the dedication of the image he set up and he ordered all the nations and languages that when the set of musical notes are rendered from his choice musical instruments they all should fall down and worship the golden images he set up. His command was furious and said that whoever did not worship his golden image when the musical notes are rendered from his choice instruments, will be cast into burning fiery furnace.

However, the servants of the highest God, the God of Israel, Father of our Lord Jesus Christ, did just the opposite. The three Jews, Shadrach, Meshach, and Abednego did neither worship the golden image which the king set up nor worship his gods.

The king rose in rage and in his fury commanded to bring Shadrach, Meshach, and Abednego before him for questioning. The king questioned as to whether it is true that they did not worship and serve his gods and do not bow down to the golden image he had set up.

The king gave them another chance to worship the image that he had set up, and warned them that if they defied his command they will be thrown into the fiery burning furnace. He took pride in his gods and challenged as to which God could deliver them from his anger and their consequent death.

Shadrach, Meshach, and Abednego, however, boldly said to the king that they do not care for the king's command when it comes to serving the living God.

They trusted and declared to the king that the God whom they serve is able to not only deliver them from the burning fiery furnace but also from the king's hand. They also asserted that even if the living God does not deliver them from the burning fiery furnace, they willingly accept the death rather than serving idols.

King Nebuchadnezzar came to know from Chaldeans that Shadrach, Meshach and Abednego defied his command and did not bow down to the idol he made nor did they worship it. This angered the king and commanded that they should be cast into burning fiery furnace heated up seven times more than it was. He commanded mightiest of men in the land of Babylon to bind them and cast into the burning fiery furnace. They bound Shadrach, Meshach and Abednego with their clothes on into the burning fiery furnace.

Because the furnace was too hot seven times greater than it was to be the mighty men who bound Shadrach, Meshach, and Abednego and cast them into the furnace, were burnt alive; however, God protected Shadrach, Meshach and Abednego even when they were in the midst of the fire.

Nebuchadnezzar not only saw them alive and waling in the midst of fire, but he saw an additional one along with them making a total of four men walking in the midst of the furnace. The king was surprised that none of the four were hurt by the fire.

Nebuchadnezzar came near the mouth of the burning fiery furnace and called Shadrach, Meshach and Abednego to come out of the fire asserting that they were the servants of the highest God. They came out of the fire unharmed by the fire and to the surprise of princes, governors, captains, king's counsellors. They all saw that fire had no power over these three men. Leave along burning of clothes, they did not even smell of fire on their clothes or bodies.

Nebuchadnezzar, after witnessing this great miracle, said "Blessed be the God of Shadrach, Meshach, and Abednego". He acknowledged that their God sent angel and delivered them. He made a decree that if any of the people, nations, and languages, spoke any ill of the God of Shadrach, Meshach and Abednego, will be cut into pieces and their houses shall be made dunghill.

Nebuchadnezzar acknowledged that there is none like their God, who could deliver them from such danger as from the burning fiery furnace. The king promoted Shadrach, Meshach and Abednego in the land of Babylon.

(From Daniel 3:1-30)

# CHAPTER 18
# THE FOLLY OF IDOLATRY

Psalmist and Isaiah showed how wrong it is to worship idols. They are made of men out of the material created by God.

A sure contrast is evident between the living God and the idols and the advantages and the disadvantages of worshipping them. A stark contrast is seen in them as it is exposed by the Psalmist in Psalm 135 and Prophet Isaiah.

The psalmist advises the priests, who stood before the LORD, to praise Him and exalt His name above all names because the LORD is Almighty and it is pleasant to do so.

The LORD chose Israel as His nation and as His peculiar treasure. From the victories and sustenance He has given them it can said with no doubt that He is great above all other gods. He did in heaven, on earth and in the seas, whatsoever it pleased Him according to His sovereign pleasure.

The LORD causes vapors to rise from the ends of the earth and causes lightening when it rains. He has in His storehouses the winds that He sends onto the earth at His will and man does not know where they come from and where they go.

The LORD sends hurricanes and tornadoes to chastise the unruly and ungodly and in contrast He sends quite winds and perennial rains to the land where His people worship Him. Science would forecast to a great extent but not surely the origin, the finest details, the direction and the intensity of the wind. "The wind bloweth where it listeth, and thou hearest the sound thereof, but canst not tell whence it cometh, and whither it goeth: so is every one that is born of the Spirit" (John 3:8)

Neither science nor man could stop the damaging winds that come as a result of the LORD's fury when He sends them to chasten mankind. The Lord has full command over storms and winds and rebukes them to calm down. "And he saith unto them, Why are ye fearful, O ye of little faith? Then he arose, and rebuked the winds and the sea; and there was a great calm" (Matthew 8:26)

Pharaoh's heart was hardened and he would not let go the LORD's treasured possession, the children of Israel, and then the LORD's anger was kindled against them and He killed the first born of Pharaoh, and of every Egyptian and of their cattle. He caused the best of Pharaoh's chariots, horses and horsemen to drown and die in the Red Sea. Israel rejoiced at the marvelous victory the LORD gave them over Egyptians when they walked on the dry land in the midst of the Red Sea to the other side of the sea, safely, while Pharaoh's army sunk into its deep waters.

While the children of Israel were on their journey to their Promised Land the LORD helped Moses and the children of Israel in slaying mighty kings and defeating their nations.

When Sihon, king of the Amorites, would not let pass the children of Israel through his land, the LORD humbled him to face utter defeat by the people of Israel.

The children of Israel not only took possession of Sihon's cities but they could comfortably pass through his regions (Cf. Numbers 21:21-24).

OG, king of Bashan, who was a giant and powerful king of Amorites and ruled over sixty cities, was defeated by Moses and his people when the LORD struck OG with His mighty hand. (Cf. Numbers 21:33-35).

The LORD gave to the children of Israel as their heritage, the land of Canaan, a land flowing with milk and honey, as their possession. The LORD's name endures forever and His name is to be praised. His memorial endures forever. Psalmist goes on to say...

"The idols of the heathen [are] silver and gold, the work of men's hands. They have mouths, but they speak not; eyes have they, but they see not. They have ears, but they hear not; neither is there [any] breath in their mouths. They that make them are like unto them: [so is] every one that trusteth in them" (Psalm 135:15-18)

The LORD blessed Israel and says to them that He formed them from the womb and, therefore, not to be afraid of anything. He assures them that there is no god except the LORD God of heavens, the God of Israel, and Jehovah is His name.

The nations with idols as their gods will not be able to do any harm to them and no weapon that is formed against them shall prosper. They that make graven images are vanity.

The idols do not see nor do they hear and they that worship them, no doubt, feel comfortable in this world but they are surely devoid of heavenly peace and short of any hope of their soul after their death.

Bible speaks of believers that they will be with the Lord for ever and ever in heaven, where there is no sorrow or pain or disease, and they walk on 'street of gold' in contrast to Satan and his followers spending their eternity, gnashing their teeth, in the lake of fire where fire and thirst do not quench (Cf. Revelation Chapters 20 to 22).

"Surely thou didst set them in slippery places: thou castedst them down into destruction" (Psalms 73:18)

The workmen who make idols are men, who with their tongs and coals, fashion them with hammers with their strength. When man is hungry and thirsty he is weak and then he eats and drinks and gains strength and with that strength he makes the graven images and calls them as his gods. The idols, which are called as man's gods, are made with the strength of man and he bows down to them seeking strength.

The carpenter stretches out his measuring tape and marks out a line and uses compass and makes a figure of a man according to the beauty of man or as he perceives his god to be like, many times much smaller than man's stature, and places them to remain static in man's house.

Man brings wood from Cedars, Cyprus and Oak and he makes firewood out of them for warming up his body or cook food for himself and he carves the wood into idols and puts them on pedestals not to move but to sit at one place.

There is the idol sitting in a cage like a bird. What profit is there to worship them that do not see or hear or move. When their gods are to be moved to a different location men carry them on their shoulders because they cannot move by themselves.

Imagine a father carrying his disabled child on his shoulder or in a wheel chair and pity on those idols when man carries them on his shoulders in a similar way from place to place. Men call them gods and the gods are carried by men. Men call them great and they are shorter than them. (Cf. Isaiah Chapters 44 and 46)

"They bear him upon the shoulder, they carry him, and set him in his place, and he standeth; from his place shall he not remove: yea, one shall cry unto him, yet can he not answer, nor save him out of his trouble" (Isaiah 46:7) The LORD God of Israel, the Father of our Lord Jesus Christ says:

"And even to your old age I am he; and even to hoar hairs will I carry you: I have made, and I will bear; even I will carry, and will deliver you" (Isaiah 46:4)

Just as the house of Israel, the house of Aaron, and the house of the Levi, who fear the LORD are asked to bless the LORD and praise His name, we are also asked to worship Him in spirit and in truth.

Individual saints in the Old Testament period offered sacrifices until Mosaic Law came into existence and they were priests by themselves. However, after Mosaic Law came into existence the entire congregation of children of Israel was called "Kingdom of Priests" but inasmuch as they violated the Law the Tribe of Levi was given the privilege to become priests.

Only the high priest had the access to the Most Holy place in the Tabernacle only once a year and that was on the "Day of Atonement".

Now that Lord Jesus Christ is our High Priest we all have access to the Father through Him and we are all priests of God. We are His "Royal Priesthood" and living Sacrifice. The Lord expects from us sincere worship in spirit and in truth. In lieu of sacrifices offered under Mosaic Law we are required to offer our bodies as living sacrifices (Cf. Romans 12:1, 1 Corinthians 6:15-20, 1 Peter 2:5-9)

"He that believeth on the Son hath everlasting life: and he that believeth not the Son shall not see life; but the wrath of God abideth on him" (John 3:36) Lord Jesus Christ, the Son of God, bore our sin upon Himself and died on the cross for our sake that we may be made righteous. He was buried and rose from the dead on the third day.

Whoever confesses by mouth "Jesus is the Lord" and believes in heart that God raised Him from the dead will be saved. Today is the day of salvation. Confess sins to Lord Jesus Christ and accept Him as your personal savior.

"Having therefore, brethren, boldness to enter into the holiest by the blood of Jesus, By a new and living way, which he hath consecrated for us, through the veil, that is to say, his flesh; And having an high priest over the house of God; Let us draw near with a true heart in full assurance of faith, having our hearts sprinkled from an evil conscience, and our bodies washed with pure water" (Hebrews 10:19-22)

# CHAPTER 19
# NEBUCHADNEZZAR HUMBLED

Appreciating the LORD's greatness or proclaiming laurels for Him is not the same as accepting the Lord Jesus Christ as one's personal Savior. Nebuchadnezzar had great laurels for the LORD God of Daniel, Shadrach, Meshach and Abednego after seeing miracles from the God of Israel who delivered them in dire situations.

Nebuchadnezzar called on all the peoples, nations and languages that live on the earth and wished peace to multiply on them. He went on applauding the LORD's works and wonders for them. More than anything he loudly proclaimed that the kingdom of the God of Daniel, Shadrach, Meshach and Abednego, is an everlasting kingdom and it endures from generation to generation.

If only he had not boasted of his greatness and exalting himself without realizing that the God of Israel rules over all the earth, he would have been saved from the disastrous life for seven periods of time, which is seven years of time (cf. Dan. 7:25; 12:7)

Nebuchadnezzar saw a dream that made him afraid. This dream is different from the one that he saw earlier as described Daniel Chapter 2.

In earlier case he forgot the dream which was revealed to him by Daniel by the help of living God. Daniel not only revealed the dream to the king but he also made known to the king the interpretation thereof.

The dream described in Daniel Chapter 4 was in memory of the king and it alarmed him. He called for all the wise men of Babylon, the magicians, the enchanters, the Chaldeans, and the astrologers and let them know the dream. He demanded from them the interpretation of the dream that he saw. None of them could explain the interpretation of the dream that he saw. It may be either because they were unable to explain or they may have feared of the consequences that may result in their death, because the interpretation as revealed to the king later by Daniel was to point utter destruction of his kingdom.

The last resort the king had was to call for Daniel, whom he named after his god Belteshazzar, and asked him to let him know the interpretation of the dream that he saw. When Nebuchadnezzar said to Daniel that the spirit of holy gods was in him, he was not saying the Spirit of the God Israel was in him, but he was pointing to his gods and took pride in saying that he named Daniel as Belteshazzar after the name of his god. He says Daniel was the chief of the magicians and no mystery was too hard for him to reveal.

Nebuchadnezzar revealed the dream to Daniel saying that he saw tree in the midst of the earth and its height was great. It grew strong and so tall that the people on the ends of the earth saw it. It provided food for all with the abundant fruit that grew on it while its leaves radiated their beauty. The fowl in the air found shelter in its branches while the animals rested in its shade and every living creature was fed by it.

While he was still watching the vision in his dream, Nebuchadnezzar saw a holy one coming down from heaven with the proclamation the Most High God rules kingdom of men giving it to whomsoever he pleases in and snatching it away from the proud. The holy one ordered to chop down the tree; cut off its branches and strip off its leaves and then scatter its fruit.

The Holy one ordered that the stump and the roots of that great tree fallen should be retained to help people to see that no matter how great or proud one may be, one's rise or fall is in the Almighty God. From the assertions of Nebuchadnezzar it can be deduced that he was very proud king. Although he acknowledged the greatness of the God of Daniel, yet he never yielded to accept Him as his LORD.

Mere expression of remorse or saying Jesus is good or a great prophet etc. will never fetch salvation. Even prisoners and criminals feel sorry for what they have done, but feeling sorry will not help entering into the kingdom of God. The Bible is clear that unless one is born of spirit and water and accept Lord Jesus Christ as one's personal savior, one will not enter the kingdom of God.

*"Jesus answered and said unto him, Verily, verily, I say unto thee, Except a man be born again, he cannot see the kingdom of God"* *(John 3:3)*

*"That if thou shalt confess with thy mouth the Lord Jesus, and shalt believe in thine heart that God hath raised him from the dead, thou shalt be saved. For with the heart man believeth unto righteousness; and with the mouth confession is made unto salvation" (Romans 10:9-10)*

The holy one ordered that the stump of the tree and the roots of it should be bound with a band of iron and bronze amid the tender grass of the field. Iron shows strength, while the bronze shows judgment. The strong tree is brought down and judged while the feeble grass around it is blessed.

The tender grass not only keeps smiling in happiness around the tumbled great tree, but also keeps watching how the LORD keeps the stump and the roots of the humbled tree wet with the dew of heaven.

The holy one proclaims harsh punishment on Nebuchadnezzar represented by the humbled tree that his portion will be with the beasts of the field and in the grass of the earth. Going little more in the punishment inflicted the holy one says that his capabilities and his mid be changed to that of a beast. The punishment is to cease only after seven periods of time. This punishment is inflicted on him in order that he may know that the Most High rules the kingdom of men and setting up the humble one to rule. Nebuchadnezzar asks Daniel to interpret the dream.

DANIEL INTERPRETES THE SECOND DREAM

Daniel was perplexed to listen from Nebuchadnezzar the dream. While the king assures him that there is nothing to get alarmed about the dream, Daniel proceeds to interpret the dream for the king as follows.

The huge tree that the king saw in his dream, was the king. Just as it grew great wherein there was abundant fruit, and under shade of which the beasts of the field found refuge, and in whose branches the birds lived, the kingdom of Nebuchadnezzar grew great and the great tree represented the king.

There came a decree from the King of kings, the LORD of lords to chop of the kingdom of Nebuchadnezzar, but leave the remnant of his kingdom and he will be driven out from his kingdom to make his living among the beasts of the field. The king will be made to eat grass like an ox and he shall be wet with the dew of heaven for seven periods of time passes over him, when he will recognizes that the Most High rules the kingdom of men and gives it to whomsoever He desires to give. During the seven periods of time the heaven rules the kingdom and after the designated time period is over, the kingdom will be restored to him.

Thereafter, Daniel warns the king to give up unrighteous life that he was leading, stop sinning, show mercy to the oppressed in order that he may prosper in his life for a greater time period after the kingdom is restored to him.

# CHAPTER 20
# NEBUCHADNEZZAR HUMILIATED

As Nebuchadnezzar was walking on the roof of his royal palace in Babylon at the end of twelve months the king took pride in his kingdom, and boasted saying he built the great Babylon with his mighty power as a royal residence and the glory of his majesty. While his words were still in his mouth there fell a voice from heaven saying "O King Nebuchadnezzar, to you it is spoken: The kingdom has departed from you, and you shall be driven from among men, and your dwelling shall be with the beasts of the field. And you shall be made to eat grass like an ox, and seven periods of time shall pass over you, until you know that the Most High rules the kingdom of men and gives it to whom he will." (cf. Daniel 4:29-32)

**SIMILITUDE OF KING
NEBUCHADNEZZAR HUMBLED
AFTER HIS PRIDE**

Artwork by Leslie John
© Leslie John 2017

The word from the LORD was fulfilled immediately when Nebuchadnezzar was driven from among men and ate grass like an ox does. "His body was wet with dew of heaven until his hair grew as long as eagles' feathers, and his nails were like birds' claws" (Ref. Daniel 4:33)

Inasmuch as there is no reference in secular History or in Josephus' writings of Nebuchadnezzar becoming an animal, it is widely believed that it is an allegorical reference to his loss of power and authority over his people and his hypochondriac behavior of eating grass, and behaving like an animal for seven years.

# CHAPTER 21
# NEBUCHADNEZZAR RESTORED

Seven periods of time was to complete before Nebuchadnezzar's restoration. It was ordained by Almighty God. Nebuchadnezzar was insane for seven years. However, after the lapse of the seven periods of time he regained his conscientiousness, lifted his eyes to eyes and blessed the Almighty God. He honored and praised the LORD, saying He lives forever and His dominion is an everlasting dominion. He not only repented of his pride but honored the LORD God of Israel. He acknowledged the fact that the Kingdom of the LORD God of heavens endures from generation to generation. The pride of inhabitants of the earth is reckoned as nothing. The LORD does what it pleases Him among the host of heaven and among the people of the earth. No power on earth or elsewhere can hinder the LORD's plans or desire. His arm is strong. His thoughts are above any man's thoughts. None can question the LORD as to what He was doing, or what He would do in future.

The Lord says in New Testament that the gates of hell cannot stop the Church that He was building. No matter how men may persecute Christians but the Church grows amid persecutions. It happened in the past and it will happen in future, as well.

*"And I say also unto thee, That thou art Peter, and upon this rock I will build my church; and the gates of hell shall not prevail against it" (Matthew 16:18)*

God does not tolerate the proud. He resists the proud and brings humiliation to the proud. The wise man Solomon said...

*"Pride goeth before destruction, and an haughty spirit before a fall". (Proverbs 16:18)*

It happened in the past when Proud Goliath was brought to nothing by a David, the chosen one of the Almighty God. It is God who fights for His followers. Sennacherib's army was killed by the Angel of the LORD.

*"And the LORD sent an angel, which cut off all the mighty men of valour, and the leaders and captains in the camp of the king of Assyria. So he returned with shame of face to his own land. And when he was come into the house of his god, they that came forth of his own bowels slew him there with the sword" (2 Chronicles 32:21)*

God did not spare even the beautiful angel, Lucifer when he thought of ascending "into heaven, I will exalt my throne above the stars of God: I will sit also upon the mount of the congregation, in the sides of the north" (Isaiah 14:12-13)

Man's repentance of his sins and accepting the Lord as his personal savior alone brings salvation to him. Nebuchadnezzar's reasoning and intelligence returned to him and he was restored to His kingdom only by the grace of God. His majesty and splendor returned to him. His counselors sought him and he was established in his kingdom. He received greatness far more than what he had earlier. Therefore, Nebuchadnezzar praised the Almighty God and extolled His name. He realized that the LORD is the King of heaven and all works of the LORD are right and just. The LORD will surely humble the proud.

# CHAPTER 22
# HAUGHTY BELSHAZZAR HUMBLED

Belshazzar, who was the last king of Babylon, perhaps the grandson of Nebuchadnezzar, did very wrong thing in offending the living God, the God of Daniel, Shadrach and Meshach. He drank wine and served the meals in the vessels used by the children of Israel in the Tabernacle and Solomon's Temple (cf. Exodus 25:39; Numbers 7:1; 1 Kings 8:4; 1 Kings 15:15; 2 Kings 24:13).

*"And Nebuchadnezzar carried part of the vessels of the house of Jehovah to Babylon, and put them in his temple at Babylon" (2 Chronicles 36:7)*

The vessels were very sacred and were consecrated for the use in God's service by the High Priest. Nebuchadnezzar had removed those vessels from Solomon's Temple when he invaded the "kingdom of Judah", which was the Southern kingdom of Israel. The temple was in Jerusalem, which was subdued by Nebuchadnezzar, according to the plan of God because of the disobedience of the children of Israel. (cf. Exodus 30:25-30; Exodus 40:9-10).

*"And the tabernacle too and all the vessels of service he sprinkled in like manner with blood" (Hebrews 9:21)*

Belshazzar hosted a great feast to his nobles, his wives, and his concubines and it was so demeaning that the vessels which were used for God's service once were given by Belshazzar to his wives and concubines. They drank wine in those vessels. The extent of the wrath God sent upon him shows the how precious were those vessels and the service rendered to the

LORD those vessels. No doubt, the children of Israel were sent into seventy years captivity for failure to keep seventy Sabbath rests in seventy years; nevertheless, God took great exception to the usage of His precious vessels by the concubines of Belshazzar.

As if that was not enough Belshazzar and his guests greatly offended the living God by praising their "gods of gold and of silver, of brass, of iron, of wood, and of stone" while drinking wine from the precious vessels.

God is jealous and He said He will not give His glory to anyone.

*"Thou shalt not bow down thyself to them, nor serve them: for I the LORD thy God am a jealous God, visiting the iniquity of the fathers upon the children unto the third and fourth generation of them that hate me"; (Exodus 20:5)*

*"For thou shalt worship no other god: for the LORD, whose name is Jealous, is a jealous God: (Exodus 34:14)*

*"I am Jehovah, that is my name; and my glory will I not give to another, neither my praise to graven images" (Isaiah 42:8)*

While Belshazzar and his guests were making merry at the cost of insulting the God of Israel, there came fingers of man's hand, part of which was seen by the king. The part of the hand that the king saw wrote on the plaster of the wall of the king's palace, few words that perplexed him. His countenance appeared scary, troubled with disturbed thoughts while the joints of his lions were loosened, and his knees rattled one against another.

The king loudly called for his magicians, the Chaldeans, the wise men, and the astrologers and said to them that whoever interpreted his dream would be clothed with purple, signifying honor, and will be adorned with gold chain around his neck, and will be third ruler in his kingdom.

His trusted magicians, the Chaldeans, the wise men, and the astrologers could not read the writing nor could they interpret the dream for the king. While the king was had commotion in his mind the queen came to his help saying there was in his kingdom a man, who had spirit of holy gods in him.

The man who helped the Belshazzar's grandfather, was Daniel, also called Belteshazzar, who interpreted the dreams of Nebuchadnezzar in almost a similar situation. Daniel was, therefore, made the master of magicians. The context reads as if Nebuchadnezzar was Belshazzar's father, but the reference was similar to that of reference of David to Lord Jesus, where David was called the father of Jesus (cf. Luke 1:32)

At the behest of the queen the king summoned Daniel to interpret the king's dream. The king inquired if Daniel could interpret the dream for him. He also said that his trusted magicians, the Chaldeans, the wise men, and the astrologers could neither read nor understand the writing on the wall by the hand. The king promised Daniel that he would clothe him in purple clothes, and have a chain of fold around his neck and will make him the third ruler in his kingdom.

Daniel honored God and said to the king to keep his gifts for himself and give them to some other man. However, he said he would interpret the king's dream, because he had confidence in his God the Almighty.

Daniel said to the king that the Almighty God gave Nebuchadnezzar the kingdom, greatness, glory and majesty in such abundance that all peoples, nations, and languages trembled before him. Nebuchadnezzar would slay whom he would and keep alive whom he would want to keep alive. He would exalt whom he would want to, and humble one, whom he would want to humble. His pride grew great and boasted of his capability of building Babylon by himself.

It was then that Almighty God brought him so low that he became like an animal with heart and mind like that of an animal. He ate just as animals ate. He was driven from his throne of his kingdom to live with beasts of the field, and wild donkeys. His body was bathed in dew from heaven until he knew that Almighty God, the God of Israel, rules the whole earth and the inhabitants thereof, and the LORD appoints to great positions whom He would want to and deposes whom He would want to.

Daniel points to the folly of Belshazzar and says to him that he was no better a man than his grandfather Nebuchadnezzar. He says to the king that he has lifted up himself against the Lord of heavens, and he and his nobles, his wives, and his concubines drank wine in the sacred vessels used by Moses and Aaron in the Tabernacle, and later by the priests in Solomon's Temple. As if that was not enough, they all praised idols, their gods made of lifeless gold, of silver, of brass, of iron, of wood, and of stone, which have neither eyes to see, nor ears to hear, or knowledge. He defied the God of heavens, in whose hands was his breath, just as any man's breath is in the hands of the Lord.

Daniel by the help of the living God interpreted the dream for the king. He said it was because he did not honor the living God that the Lord God sent the part of the hand that wrote on the plaster of the wall of the king's palace, the words "MENE,

MENE, TEKEL, UPHARSIN". He said the interpretation of the word "MENE" is that God has numbered the days of his kingdom and finished it. He said the interpretation of the word "TEKEL" was that the king was weighed in God's balance and the LORD God found him wanting; and the interpretation of the word "UPHARSIN" was that his kingdom is divided and given to Medes and Persians.

Belshazzar fulfilled his promise to Daniel by clothing him purple clothes, by putting a golden chain around his neck and making a proclamation that Daniel is made the third ruler in the kingdom of Babylon.

The end of Belshazzar was as ordained by the God of heavens, the LORD God Jehovah, the Father of Lord Jesus Christ. The king of Chaldeans slew Belshazzar in the very same night after Daniel was made the third ruler in the kingdom, and Darius, the Mede received the kingdom

(From Daniel 5:1-31)

# CHAPTER 23
# DANIEL'S COMFORT AMID LIONS

According to Daniel 5:30-31 after Belshazzar's death, Darius became the king of Medes when he was of sixty two years of age. Darius was believed to be the same man, whose name was "Gubaru" in ancient documents that speak about Cyrus. He was not the son of any king but the son of a "Satrap" (Viceroy), who had the authority to appoint men to important positions. Darius, who lived from circa 550-486 BC, was also known as the "Darius the great". His reign was from circa 522 to 486 BC.

Darius appointed in his kingdom, a hundred and twenty satraps, signifying that his kingdom was pretty big one. He appointed three presidents to oversee the satraps. Among these three presidents Daniel excelled in his intelligence, and performance and gathered the affection of the king. He excelled in every field because God's excellent spirit was in Him.

Daniel Chapter 6 describes a wonderful story about Darius and Daniel. Daniel was beloved of the LORD God of Israel, and the Almighty God's power and wisdom was in him. He prayed to God regularly and sought the help from the LORD every day. He honored God and gave pre-eminence to Him in all aspects of His life. He never took pride in His achievements, but he always gave thanks and praises to God. He depended on God and He acknowledged God's help and His presence in his life.

Children like Daniel's story because they see God's presence in Daniel's life and His protection and rescue from the lions. Adults like this story because it shows how jealousy exists among people who are in authority. The story also shows how futile it is for a king do trust in his own power without depending on God's help. His predecessors have already seen the disaster they encountered by not honoring the living God. Nebuchadnezzar was humbled beyond anyone's imagination. God humbled him and showed to him that it is the living God who raises one and humbles one. It is the LORD who rules everyone and every kingdom. Nebuchadnezzar was restored to his normal life only after realizing this fact. Like Nebuchadnezzar Darius was also humbled by God that he may realize that God rules, and not man.

Darius was the last king in Medo-Persian reign. He faced utter defeat from Alexander the Great. As for Alexander the great, he also died of a terrible diseases in his thirties. Thus it is seen in the lives of men of authority and ordinary people that God rules. Goliath was humbled by God's chosen shepherd boy David. There is no dearth of such examples in the Bible to show that God rules.

Daniel was one of the three presidents over one hundred and twenty satraps. The two other presidents were quite jealousy over the success Daniel in the kingdom of Babylon under Darius. Without consulting Daniel they went and proposed a vile plan to the king to execute. Their aim was to destroy Daniel. They were not reluctant to tell king that all the three presidents had one opinion in their plan.

The plan, the two other presidents proposed to Darius, was that everyone in the kingdom of Babylon should petition to Darius of any need, and anyone seeking help form any other god would be cast into the den of lions.

The two presidents knew that except for a reason of a commandment to be violated from the Law of God, Daniel would not fail in any test they may subject him to. Daniel had been found excellent in every aspect of his life, and loyal to the king and in his own duties as one of the three presidents. More than the other two presidents, Daniel who was one among the three presidents chosen to help the king, Daniel was found to be more reliable and effective. God was with Daniel at all times, and that was the reason why he has successful in all that he did. He was faithful in all that he did. He was neither found wanting nor was there any error or fault in his work. There was no lack of efficiency in his work. That was the basic reason why other two presidents to trap into a failure of the king's command.

It is all jealousy that pervades mankind that brings harm not only to themselves but also to the society. They went to Darius the king and said to lied to him that all the governors of the kingdom, the administrators, satraps, the counsellors, have in unison decided that a request be made to the king that he sign a decree concerning submitting petitions to king. They went in all praises for the king and flattered him insomuch that the king yielded to their request and signed a decree that whoever petitions any god or man for thirty days other than the king will be cast into the den of lions. The strength of the decree was such that once it is established no one, including the king, cannot change the decree for any reason. Their flattery of king that appeared as if the king would become god for thirty days, resulted in the king yielding to their request, and establishing the decree.

Daniel was in quite a great deal of confrontational test of loyalties. His dilemma was that whether he should serve his God and be loyal to the LORD or to the king whom he is serving faithfully. It is hard for a man to decide in such circumstances, unless the man is a staunch believer in God, and determination to keep God's laws. Daniel was not disloyal to the king nor was he unfaith to the king at any time.

By obeying to keep God's laws and faithful to the LORD he was honestly keeping himself pure in the sight of God undaunted of consequences. He was loyal to the king in all respects but when it came to his personal beliefs he had to give priority to His God and followed his convictions. Bible says give to Caesar that which belongs to Caesar and give to God that which belongs to God. Daniel complied with both the commandments.

- Daniel did neither increase the frequency of his prayer not did he lessen the frequency. He prayed to God as was the custom since early days.
- He gave thanks to his God prayed in his upper room opening the window toward Jerusalem and praying toward Jerusalem and the Temple.
- This signifies Daniel's devotion of remembering the place of sacrifice even when there was no sacrifice there.
- On the occasion of the inauguration of Solomon's Temple King Solomon petitioned to the Almighty God, that if the LORD's people prayed turning toward Jerusalem and toward the Temple their prayers may be answered by the LORD (cf. 1 Kings 8:31-40). God honored Solomon's petition and said to Solomon...

  *"If my people, which are called by my name, shall humble themselves, and pray, and seek my face, and turn from their wicked ways; then will I hear from heaven, and will forgive their sin, and will heal their land. Now mine eyes shall be open, and mine ears attend unto the prayer that is made in this place. For now have I chosen and sanctified this house that my name may be there forever:*

*and mine eyes and mine heart shall be there perpetually".*
*(2 Chronicles 7:14-16)*

Daniel knelt down on his knees and prayed to the LORD three times a day. Kneeling down and praying signifies one's obedience to God and submitting supplication by humbling oneself and exalting God. Lord Jesus knelt down and prayed as we read in Luke 22:41, Stephen knelt down and cried in loud voice to the Lord Jesus Christ. Peter knelt down and prayed for Tabitha and she rose from the dead. Apostle Paul knelt down and prayed as we read in Acts 20:36, and there are many more!

Daniel's opponents found him pray to the living God and submitting his supplications to the LORD. It displeased the king very much that Daniel, according to two other presidents, was submitting his petitions to his God rather than to the king. It is very interesting that although the king signed the decree, yet he realized later that he was at fault. It was not a thing to have been done and, therefore, his heart did pant for sympathy towards Daniel. He was displeased with himself.

Many a time we too make such foolish decisions and then later repent. In such circumstances God honors ours repentance and provides mercifully for our needs. Darius worked hard to let Daniel go free but his own decree and the conditions laid down in the law books of Medes and Persians prevented him taking any other stance than that he already took.

The two other presidents lost no time in approaching the king to remind the provisions of the decree he signed. They questioned the king if he did not sign the decree, and if he established the decree he is bound by the law to implement it and cast Daniel into the den of lions. The king answered and said his decree stands fast and is true according to the law of the Medes and Persians. It cannot be revoked. Then they pointed Daniel's disregard to the decree and said to him that Daniel prayed to his God three times a day.

The king failed in his attempts to rescue Daniel from the foolish decree he made and delivered him to be cast into the den of lions. He tried to console Daniel saying the God of Daniel will save him. Daniel was cast into the den of lions and the stone that was laid against the den of lions was sealed with his signet, and with the signet of nobles.

The king fasted whole night and preferred to stay away from his concubines. He suffered insomnia the whole night and at dawn he rushed in haste to the den of lions. Standing at the mouth of the den of lions he cried aloud to Daniel and inquired from Daniel if his God saved him from the mouths of lions.

Daniel answered the king and wished him well first; and then said to him that his God sent an angel into the den of lions where he did lay in the midst of lions, and caused the angel to shut the mouth of the lions. The lions were incapacitated from doing any harm the servant of the LORD. Daniel said to the king that he was innocent before the king and before God. He said he did not hurt anyone.

The king was exceedingly glad that Daniel was alive and his God protected and rescued from the sure death. He commanded that Daniel be removed from the den of lions and he saw that he was not hurt in any manner. The king then, commanded that all those men who lodged complaints against Daniel, and all their wives and their children, be brought and cast into the den of lions. The hungry lions showed their mastery over the people who fell into the den of lions and before they touched the floor of the den of lions they broke their bones into pieces and had sumptuous meal.

Darius wrote unto all peoples, nations, and languages who live on the earth and wished them peace. He then made a decree that everyone in every dominion of his kingdom should fear before the God of Daniel. The king acknowledged that the God of Daniel is the living God. The reason why he wished so was basically to see that his kingdom may not be destroyed and his dominion may remain until the end. The king acknowledged that the God of Daniel is the true God, who works wonders and signs in heavens and on earth. He also acknowledged that God of Daniel delivered Daniel from the power of the fierce lions.

It is because God was with Daniel, he prospered in the reign of Darius and in the reign of Cyrus the Persian (cf. Daniel 6:1-28).

## PRAY FOR THE RULERS

*"I exhort therefore, that, first of all, supplications, prayers, intercessions, and giving of thanks, be made for all men; For kings, and for all that are in authority; that we may lead a quiet and peaceable life in all godliness and honesty. For this is good and acceptable in the sight of God our Saviour"* (1 Timothy 2:1-3)

*"Let every soul be subject unto the higher powers. For there is no power but of God: the powers that be are ordained of God. Whosoever therefore resisteth the power, resisteth the ordinance of God: and they that resist shall receive to themselves damnation. For rulers are not a terror to good works, but to the evil. Wilt thou then not be afraid of the power? do that which is good, and thou shalt have praise of*

the same: *For he is the minister of God to thee for good. But if thou do that which is evil, be afraid; for he beareth not the sword in vain: for he is the minister of God, a revenger to execute wrath upon him that doeth evil". (Romans 13:1-4)*

## LORD JESUS SAID...

*And fear not them which kill the body, but are not able to kill the soul: but rather fear him which is able to destroy both soul and body in hell. (Matthew 10:28)*

*"...Then saith he unto them, Render therefore unto Caesar the things which are Caesar's; and unto God the things that are God's". (Matthew 22:21)*

# CHAPTER 24
# GOD PROVIDES

"But rise, and stand upon thy feet: for I have appeared unto thee for this purpose, to make thee a minister and a witness both of these things which thou hast seen, and of those things in the which I will appear unto thee" (Acts 26:16)

Standing in the witness box before king Agrippa, Apostle Paul recalls God's calling of him when he was on the road to Damascus to persecute Christians. He says he heard a voice from heaven as to why he was persecuting the Lord. It was surprising! If Christians are persecuted the offenders are touching the apple of the eye of the Lord Jesus.

Apostle Paul was persecuting Christians and was heading to Damascus to persecute more and this was hurting Lord Jesus Christ personally.

Clearly the voice of Lord Jesus Christ was questioning Apostle Paul, erstwhile Saul, as to why he was persecuting. Added to that the voice warned him that it is hard for him to kick against the pricks.

The voice said to Paul the then Saul that the voice was of Lord Jesus whom he was persecuting (cf. Acts 9:5, 26:14, 15). Paul says Jesus appeared to him for a purpose and that purpose was to make him a minister of the Gospel of Jesus Christ to the Gentiles. He was called to be a witness of the things that he saw and of the things that he would see in which Jesus would appear to him.

Prophet Isaiah said that the word that goes out from the mouth of the LORD God shall not return to the LORD void, but will accomplish the things that God purposed to accomplish. He does what He pleases and His Word prospers in the thing whereunto the LORD sent it (Isaiah 55:11)

When God purposes that those calling on him should be protected, no evil power can be successful in its venture.

"For my thoughts are not your thoughts, neither are your ways my ways, saith the LORD" (Isaiah 55:8)

No matter how man tries to manipulate situations to drift from the plans of the sovereign God, the ultimate victory will be of the LORD, who sends forth His Word to accomplish His purpose. His purposes get fulfilled exactly as the LORD wishes them to be. It is man in his weakness who stumbles upon his hope. Man may get exasperated in the midst of turmoil or tribulation, but the scripture says everything works for good for those who are called according to His purpose. When man takes refuge in the LORD obeying His commandments and keep His statutes, he will get out of trouble. God is gracious, and longsuffering. His mercy endures forever. Trust and obey Him. Confess Jesus as Lord and believe in heart that God raised him from the dead on the third day; and that is all needed to be saved.

The number of individuals who got hurt in the shipwreck was two hundred and seventy six (Acts 27:37) and yet not one of them lost his life. Every one of them reached the shore in one way or the other. What a great daunting task it was on the part of the sailors to jump into sea and swim to the shore, either on the boards of the ship or the broken parts of the ship!

In such challenging situation Paul advised them contrary to their own plan. Their plan was to cast small boats and escape from the perishing ship; but Paul said to them that unless they all remain in the ship none of them will live. In addition, he asked them to take food and be courageous. Paul exhorted them to be of good cheer encouraging them that none will lose his life because the angel of the Lord stood by him and said to him that God's plan was that he should be brought before Caesar.

Paul said that not even a single hair of them will fall from their heads and asked them to eat food and stay healthy. Paul broke bread and he gave thanks to God and gave to them and they all ate it.

The shipmen thought unless they escape from the ship they would not survive but Paul said to them that unless they remain in the ship they would not survive. Paul's exhortation prevailed. (Acts 27:12-44)

Seek ye the LORD while he may be found, call ye upon him while he is near: (Isaiah 55:6)

Acts Chapter 28 begins with the details of the sailors who escaped from the shipwreck and survived their sure death. God helped Paul that he may be a witness of Him at Rome. God showed compassion on those who accompanied Paul and everyone who accompanied him escaped from death. Total number of prisoners and soldiers that escaped death was two hundred seventy six and every one of them escaped to an island called "Melita" which was also known as "Malta". While Paul and others were on their way to Rome, God stopped them at Malta to facilitate people there that they may listen to the word of God. Contrary to the common belief that those who do not understand our language and believe in superstitions would not be helpful to us God had a way to show to us through Paul that others are courteous too and receptive to the word of God. Paul showed miracles of God among the people at Malta that did not know God and prayed for them that they may see the greatness of God.

The people in Malta did not understand the language of the sailors and yet they were kind enough to Paul and all others who escaped to Malta. They kindled fire and helped them to warm themselves in that bad weather. Even though there were two hundred and seventy six of them to do the work, Apostle Paul humbled himself to gather a bundle of sticks and laid them on the fire. As they were warming themselves a venomous viper came out from the fire and stuck on Paul's hand. The viper did not just touch him or move around his hand but it wound itself hard on Paul's hand. The people at Malta, who believed in superstitions thought that Paul was a murderer, who escaped from the sea. But as they were still thinking in those lines Paul shook off the venomous viper with much ease into the fire and suffered no harm. They wondered Paul's survival from the venomous viper that wound itself hard on his hand. They saw Paul shaking off the viper with ease into the fire. They thought that Paul would have swollen body or fallen down suddenly but they saw that Paul did not suffer any harm. No surprise they thought Paul was a god.

From among them was the chief of the island, whose name was Publius, who received Paul and his company of prisoners and soldiers and treated them courteously. Paul had the opportunity to pray for the father of Publius and lay hands on him when he was sick with fever and of a bloody flux. Paul's prayer was answered and the father of Publius was healed.

After seeing this miracle many who were suffering from various diseases in that island came to Paul, who prayed for them and they were healed. The islanders were very courteous to Paul and others with him and gave many gifts to them that were necessary for them. They started again to sail after three months in a ship of Alexandria and they came to Syracuse where they stayed for three days. With the help of compass they went to Rhegium and the next day they came to Puteoli, where they found brethren.

A point to note here is that there were brethren who were believers that were perhaps Jews that heard the Gospel even before Apostle Paul went to that place called Puteoli. They desired that Paul and others should stay with them for seven days. Paul did not take pride in his work here, yet the point was that nobody can take pride in himself that unless he preaches God's word the word of God does not reach a place or person. God has His own ways to find people for him. Even before Paul preached the Gospel at Puteoli there were believers at that place. (Acts 28:1-14)

When Elijah took pride in himself saying that he was all alone left to work for God, he was told by God that God had reserved seven thousand who did not bow their heads to Baal.

"Yet I have left me seven thousand in Israel, all the knees which have not bowed unto Baal, and every mouth which hath not kissed him". (1 Kings 19:18)

"Hide me from the secret counsel of the wicked; from the insurrection of the workers of iniquity" Psalm 64:2

Apostle Paul was still a prisoner as we read in Acts Chapter 27 and he was to be brought before Caesar. God's purposes will never fail no matter what man plans to do or what hurdles one might encounter. The charge of taking Paul and other prisoners was given to a Centurion named Julius. Paul was arrested on false charges and ever since he was arrested he was defending that he was preaching the word of the living God. God not only delivered Paul from the shipwreck but others accompanying Paul also escaped death. The ship in which they were sailing had a wreck and broke into pieces but none in the ship lost life.

"And we were in the ship, all the souls, two hundred and seventy-six". (Acts 27:37) Every one of the two hundred seventy six people who were onboard the ship was saved. It was in the plan of God that Paul be brought before Caesar and it was done according to the purposes of God. Julius, the Centurion was kind to Paul, yet he refused to pay heed to the wise words of Paul not to venture out on sailing from 'Fair Havens' where they were resting for a while. The wind was contrary, but when the Centurion and others saw that south wind blew softly they gave credence to the master and the owner of the ship.

Paul had forewarned them that the voyage will be with much loss and damage, yet the Centurion and others took counsel among themselves and the master of the ship for granted. Not much time had elapsed when they all encountered a violent tempest which resulted in the ship getting uncontrollable. They sailed further and their final arrival at a place got their ship stuck in the creek. The front portion of the ship got firmly stuck in the creek and the rear portion broke into pieces.

The shipmen and others tried to escape from the boat, but Paul advised them contrary that they all should stay in the ship if they want their lives to be saved. The soldiers tried to kill those who were onboard the ship but Paul stood firm that they should not kill any one. Finally Centurion heard the words of Paul and commanded that those who knew swimming should cast themselves first into the sea and swim out to the land, and the rest should swim out to the land holding fast the broken pieces of the ship.

Notice that God's plan through his servant prevailed and the counsel of the human beings failed. They had rescue boats to escape but could not be used. They planned to kill the sailors but failed. They saw south wind blew softly and were impatient and put their plans at work and suffered loss and damage. They refused the counsel of the spirit-filled God's servant and took the counsel of the worldly and reaped bad consequences.

"I have fought a good fight, I have finished my course, I have kept the faith" 2 Timothy 4:7

# CHAPTER 25
# PAUL COMFORTS

"But after long abstinence Paul stood forth in the midst of them, and said, Sirs, ye should have hearkened unto me, and not have loosed from Crete, and to have gained this harm and loss. And now I exhort you to be of good cheer: for there shall be no loss of any man's life among you, but of the ship". (Acts 27:21-22)

After few days Paul stood in the midst of them and reminded them that they should have hearkened to his words of caution that he gave them earlier when he tried to prevent them starting on this venture in the bad weather.

Nevertheless, in that present circumstances he comforted them that they should not fear and said that an angel of the Lord stood by him saying none onboard the ship will lose his life because Paul was to be brought before Caesar.

They had to wait patiently for an answer for fourteen days even after Paul comforting them. The shipmen guessed that they were near some country and the depth of waters was twenty fathoms.

They sailed forward and guessed that the depth of the sea was about fifteen fathoms. With the increase in their fear that the ship would hit rocks they cast anchors out of the stern and waited for the day to dawn.

The shipmen thought of escaping from the ship but Paul said to the centurion that unless they remained in the ship they would not survive. The soldiers cut off the ropes of the boats to let the boats fall off from the ship into the waters.

But as they saw the day light Paul asked them to eat and be of good cheer. Paul also assured that not a single person will lose any of their hair because according to God's purpose he was to be brought before Caesar. For the sake of Paul everyone onboard the ship that is two hundred and seventy six were saved from dying.

When it was day they did not know the place where they were in and as they were trying further to sail forward they saw a creek with shore and they thought they would make it to that place safely. But when they took off the anchors and loosened the rudder bands they fell into a place where two seas met.

The front portion of the ship was stuck and the rear portion of the ship was broken because of the violent winds. The soldiers were counseling to kill the prisoners to avoid them escape from the ship, but Paul stood strongly against their counsel.

The centurion willing to save Paul commanded that those who could swim should jump into the sea and get to the land and the rest of them some on boards and some on broken pieces of the ship reached the shore. Every one of the total number two hundred and seventy six reached the land safely. (Acts 27:1-44)

1. It was evident from Acts Chapter 27 that God's providence for Apostle Paul and his mission was great.

2. It was in the plan of God that Caesar should hear the word of God.

3. Where it was very hard for people in higher position to hear the word of God, He makes ways to reach His word to them through His servants.

4. The advice of the servant filled with Holy Spirit is very valuable.

5. God had compassion on all those who were with Paul sailing to Italy.

6. None of the two hundred and seventy six lost their lives even inspite of the shipwreck wherein the ship broke into pieces.

7. The angel of the Lord stood by Paul and spoke to him that none of the sailors would lose their lives.

8. In spite of adverse situation God's servant, Paul, comforted them asking them to be of good cheer and eat.

9. Not only Centurion but every one hearkened finally to the words of Paul and escaped from death.

10. They all reached the shore.

# CHAPTER 26
# APOSTLE PAUL RESCUED

## THE SHIPWRECK

"And when it was determined that we should sail into Italy, they delivered Paul and certain other prisoners unto one named Julius, a centurion of Augustus' band" (Acts 27:1)

Through the meditation of the shipwreck in which Apostle Paul and those who were with him suffered there are few lessons to be learnt. In Acts Chapter 27 there is a description as to how Apostle Paul, who was arrested on false charges, while he was preaching the Gospel of Jesus Christ, was rescued.

Not only was he delivered by God from the peril of losing his life but all others who were with him were saved from losing their lives.

Few points to be considered are:

That Paul was surely to be taken to stand before Caesar according to God's Plan

The centurion treated Paul with kindness even though Paul was a prisoner and he was the custodian of Paul on their journey to Italy.

The Centurion and majority gave importance to the words of the master and the owner of the ship rather than the Spirit-filled Paul.

The Centurion and others gave credence to ill-advised counsels among themselves contrary to Paul's advice and suffered consequences.

At one point the Centurion refused to hear the words of Paul but ultimately he gave into the words of Paul.

Apostle Paul was arrested on false charges as he was preaching the Gospel of Jesus Christ. As per the narration in Acts Chapter 27

Paul was still a prisoner and was to be taken stand before Caesar. Along with him were Luke, the historian who wrote the Gospel of Luke and also Acts of Apostles. Also along with them were other prisoners heading to Italy.

A centurion named Julius was given charge to take care of Paul and others while on their way to Italy. Julius entreated Paul courteously and gave liberty for him to be with his friends for refreshing himself. Because the winds were contrary they sailed to Cyprus and while they were on their way they arrived at a city called Myra in Lycia.

The centurion found a ship of Alexandria sailing into Italy and he boarded them on that ship. They all arrived at a place called "Fair havens". They spent much time there and realized that sailing was dangerous.

Paul admonished them that he perceived that the voyage will bring much loss and damage. The centurion did not pay heed to the wise words of the Holy Spirit from Paul, who was a prisoner in his sight but rather took the advice of the master and the owner of the ship. The majority stood by Centurion, who believed the word of the master and the owner of the ship rather than the wise advice from God's servant. Eventually, they sailed forward even in spite of Paul's advice to the contrary.

There was a small respite in the inclement weather causing the Centurion and others onboard the ship to take a decision to move forward. Because the south wind blew softly they sailed to Crete against the advice of the word of God.

It was against the will of God that they proceeded further. Their decision to go forward was in violation to the forewarning from the Spirit filled servant of God. Paul foresaw clearly the impending danger and yet they chose to pay heed to their own convictions rather then the convictions from the living God.

Therefore thus saith the Lord GOD, Behold, I lay in Zion for a foundation a stone, a tried stone, a precious corner stone, a sure foundation: he that believeth shall not make haste. (Isaiah 28:16)

They were impatient and suffered. Isaiah 28:16 says not make haste but to wait on the Lord

They listened to the advice from majority. Majority would work in the secular world but in the sight of God the advice from the servant of God is very important even if he is single.

There was a majority who cried that Barabbas should be released in preference to the innocent Jesus. Pilate yielded to the cry of majority and delivered Jesus to the crowds to be crucified.

They assumed that soft wind would help them out and it was pleasing to them, but the advice from God's servant was contrary to their counsel.

They sought comfort in their own counsels because the destination was not far away and everything seemed to be good for them. They went against the word of God and suffered.

The result of their bad choice was that they fell victim to the shipwreck as the tempest was very violent they suffered loss. The consequence of their bad choice was that they were caught in a tempestuous wind called "Euroclydon".

The ship could not be controlled and they were constrained to let the ship go in the direction the tempest took it. When they reached Clauda they tried to unloosen the small boats to facilitate the sailors to escape.

Because the ship was greatly tossed in the tempest and as the days passed by they threw away great deal of material from off their ship. They did not see sun or stars which caused worry in them and were seeking ways to escape from the ship.

After few days Paul stood in the midst of them and reminded them that they should have hearkened to his words of caution that he gave them earlier when he tried to prevent them starting on this venture in the bad weather.

Nevertheless, in that present circumstances he comforted them that they should not fear and said that an angel of the Lord stood by him saying none onboard the ship will lose his life because Paul was to be brought before Caesar.

They had to wait patiently for an answer for fourteen days even after Paul comforting them. The shipmen guessed that they were near some country and the depth of waters was twenty fathoms. They sailed forward and guessed that the depth of the sea was about fifteen fathoms.

With the increase in their fear that the ship would hit rocks they cast anchors out of the stern and waited for the day to dawn. The shipmen thought of escaping from the ship but Paul said to the centurion that unless they remained in the ship they would not survive. The soldiers cut off the ropes of the boats to let the boats fall off from the ship into the waters.

But as they saw the day light Paul asked them to eat and be of good cheer. Paul also assured that not a single person will lose any of their hair because according to God's purpose he was to be brought before Caesar. For the sake of Paul everyone onboard the ship that is two hundred and seventy six were saved from dying.

When it was day they did not know the place where they were in and as they were trying further to sail forward they saw a creek with shore and they thought they would make it to that place safely.

However, when they took off the anchors and loosened the rudder bands they fell into a place where two seas met. The front portion of the ship was stuck and the rear portion of the ship was broken because of the violent winds.

The soldiers were counseling to kill the prisoners to avoid them escape from the ship, but Paul stood strongly against their counsel.

The centurion willing to save Paul commanded that those who could swim should jump into the sea and get to the land and the rest of them some on boards and some on broken pieces of the ship reached the shore. Every one of the total number two hundred and seventy six reached the land safely. (Acts 27:1-44)

It was evident from Acts Chapter 27 that God's providence for Apostle Paul and his mission was great.

It was in the plan of God that Caesar should hear the word of God.

Where it was very hard for people in higher position to hear the word of God, He makes ways to reach His word to them through His servants.

The advice of the servant filled with Holy Spirit is very valuable.

God had compassion on all those who were with Paul sailing to Italy.

None of the two hundred and seventy six lost their lives even inspite of the shipwreck wherein the ship broke into pieces.

The angel of the Lord stood by Paul and spoke to him that none of the sailors would lose their lives.

In spite of adverse situation God's servant, Paul, comforted them asking them to be of good cheer and eat.

Not only Centurion but every one hearkened finally to the words of Paul and escaped from death.

# CHAPTER 27
# JESUS REBUKES STORMS

"But the men marvelled, saying, What manner of man is this, that even the winds and the sea obey him!" (Matthew 8:27)

There was great multitude of people following Jesus as they saw the miracles done by Him. They saw how a leper was healed; they saw how centurion's servant was healed and they also saw Peter's mother-in-law was healed.

When Jesus touched Peter's mother-in-law, who was suffering from fever, He was not trying to diagnose her disease, nor was He trying to console her but His touching was a powerful healing-touch that healed her fully.

There was no trace of fatigue left in her nor was she feeling tired anymore but she rose up and ministered unto them.

Jesus looked at the crowd that expected more miracles from Him and said to them to go to the other side of the sea, which was "Sea of Galilee". Just before leaving to the other side of the sea He had conversation with a scribe who expressed his desire to follow Him but Jesus showed him how hard it was to follow Him.

When Jesus spoke to another he expressed his difficulty in following Him but Jesus said to him to follow Him. He said that those who are spiritually dead may go and attend to their earthly needs. Thus two different types of men were introduced to us; one that half-heartedly expressing his desire to follow Jesus and another with full of excuses when the Lord asked him to follow.

As Jesus entered the ship to go to the other side His disciples followed Him. His sailing by the sea helped future generations to have hope in the Lord that He helps those that seek His help. Jesus chose to go by sea-way instead of going by the road-way in order that His journey by the sea would be of much comfort to those who usually undertake travel by sea. It was going to be a sure sign for future sailors that they can pray to Him for their safe journey and seek His help.

Jesus was taking rest just as any human would do after tiresome job. Jesus, the Son of God, taking rest shows us that He was fully human when He was in this world. He was tired and was sleeping but He was not as deep in His sleep as Jonah was, many years ago, in the ship while trying to escape to a possible secure place from the task he was assigned. In Jesus we have our salvation and He is our redeemer.

As they were journeying there arose a vigorous tempest in the sea so much that the waves from the sea covered the ship. Indeed, everyone in the ship, except Jesus, was afraid of the tempest. Their nerves started shrinking as they saw the tempest even when the creator of the seas was right there in their midst. How often we also fear, in spite of having faith in Jesus, that some misadventure would overtake us. The Lord would have to remind us through some servant of God or through His word that He is always there with us. Indeed, He is our comfort and sustainer. It is worth recollecting Psalmist's comforting words.

"O love the LORD, all ye his saints: for the LORD preserveth the faithful, and plentifully rewardeth the proud doer. Be of good courage, and he shall strengthen your heart, all ye that hope in the LORD" (Psalms 31:23-24)

Jesus could have ordered the sea to be calm even before they started their journey or when they were sailing but He preferred not to do so and He showed that He was in control of the situation, over waters and the storms in order that His disciples may become stronger in their faith in Him. When the severity of the storm increased the disciples were afraid.

The disciples went to Lord Jesus, who was sleeping in the same ship, and awoke Him. They begged saying "Lord, save us: we perish".

They were praying for not only themselves but on behalf of all the sailors who were in the ship. They thought the storms would drown the ship.

However, they realized that the Lord of the sea was in ship, and He would be able to save them. Therefore, they prayed to Jesus to save them and Jesus heard their prayer.

Jesus admonished them that they were fearful because they lacked faith. Then He arose and rebuked the winds and sea and there was great calm. The men in the ship marveled at the miracle and wondered about the power that Jesus exercised on storms and on the winds that they obeyed His command.

Indeed Lord Jesus Christ is the Savior. Much more than the comfort that we have that our Lord has the power over storms we cast our burden on Him and rest in His arms because He gave us salvation free of cost.

While those whose sins are not forgiven and do not have Lord Jesus Christ as their savior would have to gnash their teeth in the "Lake of fire", where fire never quenches, we will be with Him for ever and ever.

"And he saith unto them, Why are ye fearful, O ye of little faith? Then he arose, and rebuked the winds and the sea; and there was a great calm" (Matthew 8:26)

# CHAPTER 28
# THE SUPERIORITY OF CHRIST

"He is the radiance of the glory of God and the exact imprint of his nature, and he upholds the universe by the word of his power. After making purification for sins, he sat down at the right hand of the Majesty on high, having become as much superior to angels as the name he has inherited is more excellent than theirs. For to which of the angels did God ever say, "You are my Son, today I have begotten you"? Or again, "I will be to him a father, and he shall be to me a son"? (Hebrews 1:3-5 ESV)

In comparison to angels, Lord Jesus was, and is always far superior to them. If Apostle Paul did not reveal this fact in the book of Hebrews, then the adherence to false teaching would have been greater than what it is now. Lord Jesus Christ is the "Son of God". The words "Son of" in the phrase "Son of God" are used to indicate the nature of God. It does not mean that Lord Jesus Christ is inferior to the Father or procreation of the Father.

Jesus said "I and the Father are one". It is hard for those who intend to argue with finite knowledge about the infinite nature of God especially with those who have their Bibles several errors in their mistranslation. They are out there determined to indoctrinate the children of God with their mistranslated Bibles that have several additions and deletions from the original writings.

They teach that Michael the Archangel became spirit-being and that spirit-being became Jesus, who is, according to them, a god. According to their false teaching Jesus is one of the many gods and salvation is achieved by doing good works.

Michael the Archangel is the highest creation of God, who said to the devil "The Lord rebuke thee" when the he disputed about the body of Moses. Michael the archangel prevailed over Satan. The devil is, obviously, not an equivalent to God but would be equal to Michael the Archangel.

Lord Jesus Christ and the Father are one. God is triune: the Father, the Son and the Holy Spirit; they are co-equal, co-existent, and yet differ in their functions.

"Yet Michael the archangel, when contending with the devil he disputed about the body of Moses, durst not bring against him a railing accusation, but said, The Lord rebuke thee". (Jude 1:9)

Many deceivers, who teach that Lord Jesus Christ did not incarnate, have gone into the world. They do not abide in the doctrine of Christ, and do not acknowledge that Lord Jesus came into this world in flesh.

"For many deceivers have gone out into the world, those who do not confess the coming of Jesus Christ in the flesh. Such a one is the deceiver and the antichrist" (2 John 1:7 ESV)

"If anyone comes to you and does not bring this teaching, do not receive him into your house or give him any greeting, for whoever greets him takes part in his wicked works" (2 John 1:10-11 ESV)

If however, one decides to listen to their teachings and debate with them it boils down to say finally to the false teachers to stick to their beliefs while we hold onto the Truth revealed in the Scriptures. We would know finally that we have wasted time debating with them.

The book of Hebrews reveals the superiority of Lord Jesus Christ over the angels. He took a position lower than angels, for a period of time, when he came into this world, in order to die a substitutionary death to save mankind from perishing. Whoever believes in Him shall not perish but have everlasting life. Salvation is by grace through faith in Him and not by doing any good works.

"Everyone who goes on ahead and does not abide in the teaching of Christ, does not have God. Whoever abides in the teaching has both the Father and the Son. (2 John 1:9 ESV)

# CHAPER 29
# PARTAKERS OF HEAVENLY CALLING

"Wherefore, holy brethren, partakers of the heavenly calling, consider the Apostle and High Priest of our profession, Christ Jesus; Who was faithful to him that appointed him, as also Moses was faithful in all his house. For this man was counted worthy of more glory than Moses, inasmuch as he who hath builded the house hath more honour than the house. For every house is builded by some man; but he that built all things is God" (Hebrews 3:1-4)

In the preceding two chapters it was established that Jesus, who is exact image of the invisible God the Father, is the Son of God, and that He is superior to angels, yet He took a position lower than that of angels for the sake of reconciling man with God. In the last two verses of Hebrews Chapter 2 a glimpse of the greatness of the Lord Jesus Christ, who is faithful High priest, is shown.

Here, in these verses there is admonition for all the believers, whom God called as brethren of Lord Jesus Christ, to take note of the heavenly blessings they are bestowed with, and of being made partakers of the heavenly calling.

There is also warning to understand that Jesus is superior to angels and Moses, and therefore, not to rebel against Him, lest they should face rigorous chastisement than those children of Israel, who left Egypt for Canaan, could not make it to the Promised Land, but perished in the wilderness. Let everyone acknowledge that inasmuch as God is the builder of the house, wherein Moses was a faithful servant, and Lord Jesus, who was the Son of God, is worthy of more glory and greater than Moses.

While God chose Israel as a nation and as His people, and Moses as their leader, Lord Jesus is the head of the Church, and He is in the midst of the Church. The Scripture gives description of Jesus.

"And he is the head of the body, the church: who is the beginning, the firstborn from the dead; that in all things he might have the preeminence. For it pleased the Father that in him should all fulness dwell; And, having made peace through the blood of his cross, by him to reconcile all things unto himself; by him, I say, whether they be things in earth, or things in heaven" (Colossians 1:18-20)

Hebrews Chapter 3 begins with word "wherefore" indicating the importance of the previous narration in chapters that believers, who had heavenly calling and having responded to that call, are blessed and became the Lord's brothers.

An interesting point next is to consider whether Jesus was an angel, or apostle or high priest. The book of Revelation shows that Jesus was the only one worthy to open the seven seals of the scroll.

Angels had different roles, and Jesus was never presented as an angel. In Chapters 1 and 2 of Hebrews, it was established undoubtedly that Jesus was not an angel, but He was greater than angels. He did not take the likeness of an angel, or lived as a Spirit being; neither did He take the likeness of anyone below in dignity than that of a man.

Lord Jesus came into this world in the likeness of man, in order to qualify Himself to purge man's sins. He said on the cross "It is finished", indicating that He finished the work assigned to Him by the Father, and thereafter ascended into heaven to sit on the right hand of the Majesty in high. It pleased the Father to bruise Him for our sake.

Seldom do we call Jesus as an apostle for the simple reason that it creates confusion and controversy in discussions. Nonetheless, in the light of few references it is not wrong to identify Jesus by the title "apostle".

"And they answered Jesus, and said, We cannot tell. And he said unto them, Neither tell I you by what authority I do these things" (Matthew 21:27)

"Then said Jesus to them again, Peace be unto you: as my Father hath sent me, even so send I you" (John 20:21)

Hebrews 3:1 is the only place in the Bible, where Jesus is called as an apostle. The word 'apostle' means 'sent'. He was sent into this world as an Ambassador from heaven. God sent His one and only Son Jesus into this world that whoever believes in Him shall not perish but have everlasting life.

Inasmuch as Lord Jesus Christ gave us a better covenant than that was in Old Testament, and also by offering His own body as sacrifice, rather than offering animals as sacrifice by the Old Testament high priest, Jesus is our High Priest.

After the fall of man he could not approach God just as he had fellowship with God in the cool of the day in the Garden of Eden. God chose priests from the tribe of Levi, and it was from among them that the mediator Moses became the leader. Subsequently Aaronic order of priesthood was established.

While daily sacrifices were offered by priests, the sacrifice for the nation of Israel could be done only by Aaron the high priest, or his descendants, who alone could enter the Holy of Holies in the Tabernacle and sprinkle the blood of Lord's goat on the mercy seat, and thereafter confess sins of the people on the scapegoat outside the Tabernacle, and from where the scapegoat was sent away to wilderness never to return again.

Greater sacrifice was made by Lord Jesus Christ. He offered His own flesh and body on the cross for our sake, and that is how He became our High Priest of the order of Melchizedek rendering easy access for every believer to approach God.

When the curtain in the Temple was rent from top to bottom by the power of the Almighty God, the privilege of worshipping and praying to the Almighty God straight in the name of Jesus Christ was given to everyone, whether of Jew or of Gentile. Jesus is our mediator and there is, therefore, no other priest is required to be in the middle between God and men. Thus Lord Jesus Christ has become superior to Moses.

"And as they were eating, Jesus took bread, and blessed it, and brake it, and gave it to the disciples, and said, Take, eat; this is my body" (Matthew 26:26)

"I am the vine, ye are the branches: He that abideth in me, and I in him, the same bringeth forth much fruit: for without me ye can do nothing." (John 15:5)

"I am crucified with Christ: nevertheless I live; yet not I, but Christ liveth in me: and the life which I now live in the flesh I live by the faith of the Son of God, who loved me, and gave himself for me" (Galatians 2:20)

# CHAPTER 30
# THE MISSION OF JESUS

"I mean that the heir, as long as he is a child, is no different from a slave, though he is the owner of everything, but he is under guardians and managers until the date set by his father. In the same way we also, when we were children, were enslaved to the elementary principles of the world. But when the fullness of time had come, God sent forth his Son, born of woman, born under the law, to redeem those who were under the law, so that we might receive adoption as sons. And because you are sons, God has sent the Spirit of his Son into our hearts, crying, "Abba! Father!" So you are no longer a slave, but a son, and if a son, then an heir through God" (Galatians 4:1-7 ESV)

## HAS GOD CASTAWAY THE CHILDREN OF ISRAEL? No!

"I ask, then, has God rejected his people? By no means! For I myself am an Israelite, a descendant of Abraham, a member of the tribe of Benjamin. God has not rejected his people whom he foreknew. Do you not know what the Scripture says of Elijah, how he appeals to God against Israel?"(Romans 11:1-2 ESV)

"For I would not, brethren, that ye should be ignorant of this mystery, lest ye should be wise in your own conceits; that blindness in part is happened to Israel, until the fulness of the Gentiles be come in" (Romans 11:25)

"But now hath he obtained a more excellent ministry, by how much also he is the mediator of a better covenant, which was established upon better promises". (Hebrews 8:6)

The Old covenants included in them the shadows of new things to come. Old Testament law was stringent in nature, and the law demanded unconditional obedience. It was hard to keep the law that is in the Old Testament. In the New Testament Godï¿½s abundant grace is available.

Man by confessing his sins to God and accepting Jesus as the Lord will receive eternal life. Repentance of sins to Jesus and accepting him as the Lord is sufficient to be saved. Lord Jesus Christ is the only mediator between man and the Father. Jesus said, in John 10:30 "I and my Father are one".

# CHAPTER 31
# REDEEMED BY HIS BLOOD

"Forasmuch as ye know that ye were not redeemed with corruptible things, as silver and gold, from your vain conversation received by tradition from your fathers; But with the precious blood of Christ, as of a lamb without blemish and without spot" (1 Peter 1:18-19)

Moses had three major roles to perform:

• To be the leader of the children of Israel

• To hand over the Law as given by God to the children of Israel and

• To mediate between the children of Israel and God.

Lord Jesus Christ came into this world as THE WAY, THE TRUTH, and THE LIFE

• To redeem man from his sin

• To give man the beatitudes as found in Matthew Chapter 5, 6 and 7 and

• To mediate between man and the Father.

Jesus gave two great commandments as found in Mark 12:30-31

"And thou shalt love the Lord thy God with all thy heart, and with all thy soul, and with all thy mind, and with all thy strength: this is the first commandment. And the second is like, namely this, Thou shalt love thy neighbour as thyself. There is none other commandment greater than these",

The two commandments given by Lord Jesus contain the essence of all the Ten Commandments, and He is our mediator between us and the Father.

Moses was the deliverer of God's children physically, while Jesus was the deliverer spiritually of His people Jews first and the Gentiles next. "But now hath he obtained a more excellent ministry, by how much also he is the mediator of a better covenant, which was established upon better promises" Hebrews 8:6

The New Testament covenant is the best of all that we could receive from Jesus. The Old covenant included in it the shadows and types of the things to come and the New Testament contains the anti-types and the substance.

Old Testament law was stringent in nature, which demanded unconditional obedience to the Law whereas the New Testament demands sincere obedience, repentance of sins to Jesus and accepting Him as the Lord. We are saved by grace through faith.

During the Old Testament period sins were not fully forgiven but they were covered when the sacrifices were offered. In Jesus, who was without any sin and without any blemish, and who became sin for us on the cross, are sins fully forgiven of all the Old Testament saints and of those in New Testament Period.

# CHAPTER 32
# INTERCESSORY PRAYER

It was of great consolation to the children of Israel that Moses chose to intercede on their behalf, because just a little while ago, before Moses interceded before the LORD, he was very much displeased with them when they made an idol and worshipped it.

When Moses returned from the Mount Sinai with two tablets written on them with the finger of God, the Ten Commandments, he saw Aaron and the children of Israel had made a calf of gold and were worshipping it. They even went to the extent of stripping themselves and worshiping the idol in their nakedness (Exodus 32:25)

Moses was very angry to look at that situation and ordered that whoever was on the Lord's side may gather on his side. The sons of Levi joined him. Moses ordered a great slaughter of their brothers and companions. The children of Levi obeyed him and there fell three thousand men.

Moses asked them to consecrate themselves to the LORD that He may bless them. On the next morning, Moses said to them that they sinned greatly and, therefore, he decided to return to the LORD to make atonement for their sins. Just as he said, Moses returned to the LORD and said to HIM that the children of Israel sinned greatly, but they should be forgiven of their sins.

"Yet now, if thou wilt forgive their sin–; and if not, blot me, I pray thee, out of thy book which thou hast written" (Exodus 32:32)

Every intercession of Moses was so powerful that the LORD repeatedly showed love and mercy on Israel. The LORD was pleased with Moses and He said to Moses that He will blot out whoever sinned, in due course of time when He visits them, but for now he may return to them and lead them.

The LORD plagued the people, because they made the calf, which Aaron made as an idol, for them. The LORD gave instructions to Moses to move on so that He could fulfill the promise He made and swore unto the Abraham, Isaac, and Jacob, that He will deliver the children of Israel from all their enemies.

The LORD promised to Moses that He will send an angel before him, and will drive out all the gentile nations — the Canaanites, the Amorites, the Hittites, the Perizzites, the Hivites and the Jubusites. The LORD called the children of Israel as "stiff necked people" (Exodus 33:3).

## THE INTERCESSORY PRAYER OF LORD JESUS CHRIST

Lord Jesus Christ's intercessory prayer was greater than that of Moses. He lifted up His eyes as He prayed in Gethsemane, and invoked the love of the Father in heaven, and sought help from Him to be always with His disciples. Just before He was crucified He prayed to the Father in Heaven that He had finished the work that He had embarked upon to finish in this world.

Lord Jesus glorified the Father and prayed that just as He had glorified the Father in heaven, He may be glorified with the glory that He had with Him even before the world was.

It is that prayer that brought us under the tender care of the Father in heaven. Jesus prayed that not only His disciples need to be protected but all those, who believed on the word through them, need to be protected. "Neither pray I for these alone, but for them also which shall believe on me through their word". (John 17:20)

Therefore, it is necessary that believers in Christ make intercessory prayers to receive help, guidance, and protection from God through His Son Jesus Christ.

# CHAPTER 33
# THE SAME SPIRITUAL DRINK

"And did all drink the same spiritual drink: for they drank of that spiritual Rock that followed them: and that Rock was Christ. But with many of them God was not well pleased: for they were overthrown in the wilderness. Now these things were our examples, to the intent we should not lust after evil things, as they also lusted" (1 Corinthians 10:4-6)

Writing to Corinthians Apostle Paul says to them that they should not be ignorant that the children of Israel, during the period of Moses, passed under the cloud, and passed through the Red sea, which signified that they were baptized unto Moses in the cloud and in the sea. They all ate the same spiritual food and drank of that spiritual Rock that followed them; and that rock was Christ.

It was when the children of Israel were redeemed from the bondage of slavery under Pharaoh in Egypt that they had their physical deliverance. Except for their doubting nature, and rebellion, they could have entered the Promised Land very quickly after coming out of Egypt; but because they murmured against the LORD again and again, they had to wander in the wilderness for forty years.

The children of Israel left wilderness of "Sin" and came to Rephidim, where there was no water for them to drink. They, who were slaves under Pharaoh for four hundred years, murmured against God. They chided with Moses and demanded water to drink. When Moses asked them as to why they were tempting the LORD, they in their thirst, retorted asking if he brought them from out of Egypt to kill them, their children and their cattle with thirst.

Moses was deeply distressed and cried to the Lord to help him know as to what he should do to the children of Israel, who were ready to stone him. The LORD answered and said to him to take with him the elders of Israel and his rod that he used to smite the river in order to turn the waters into blood, and go to the rock in Horeb.

The LORD said to Moses to smite the said rock upon which He will stand and water will come out of it that the people may drink.

Moses obeyed the LORD in the sight of the elders of Israel. Thus the children of Israel drank water from the rock. Moses called the place "Massah" (which means temptation), and "Meribah" (which means chiding or strife), because the children of Israel tempted the LORD and doubted if He was there among them or not (cf. Exodus 17:1-7)

A similar situation occurred when the children of Israel dwelt in Kadesh in the desert of "Zin", where there was no water. They gathered together and strove with Moses and Aaron and questioned if God wanted that they die in the wilderness just as their fathers died in Egypt when they were slaves.

They also questioned Moses and Aaron as to why they brought them out of the land of Egypt if their desire was not to see that their cattle die? They called the place as "evil place" and said the place had neither seed, nor figs, or vines, or pomegranates, or water to drink.

The glory of the LORD appeared to them there and the LORD spoke to Moses when Moses and Aaron went out unto the door of the Tabernacle of the congregation and fell prostrate before the LORD. The LORD said to him to take his rod, which he used for turning the river water into blood, and gather the children of Israel and Aaron, and speak to the rock before their eyes. The LORD said that the rock will give forth his water, and that Moses shall bring forth the water out of the rock and give them and their cattle to drink.

As commanded by God Moses took the rod from before the LORD. He and Aaron gathered the children of Israel before the rock and Moses spoke angrily to them and called them 'rebels'. In his anger he asked them if they should bring forth water from the rock and lifted up his hand and smote it with his rod twice.

No doubt, water came forth abundantly and the congregation and their cattle drank from the rock; but the act of Moses was highly displeasing to the LORD.

The LORD knew the needs of His people and provided water to them and their cattle; but the anger of Moses towards the children of Israel seemed to be greater than the displeasure of the LORD towards the children of Israel. God counted the violation by Moses of His command as very serious disobedience.

There was reason why the LORD said to Moses to speak to the rock rather than strike it. First time, when they were at Rephidim the LORD said Moses to smite the rock and it gave water but second time when they were at Kadesh in the desert of Zin the LORD said to Moses to speak to the rock and it will give forth his water; but alas! Moses smote it. That Rock was

Christ and He was to be smitten only once, in future, while in his incarnation as Savior.

When Moses smote the Rock the Lord, the intended purpose was not shown to the people of Israel and he did not sanctify the LORD in the midst of the children of Israel.

"Because ye trespassed against me among the children of Israel at the waters of Meribah-Kadesh, in the wilderness of Zin; because ye sanctified me not in the midst of the children of Israel" (Deuteronomy 32:51)

Later, speaking to Joshua, Moses recollected his error. He said the LORD did not accept his repentance because his disobedience was great and it projected a wrong meaning to the offer that the LORD made. The LORD said to him that he shall not go over Jordan and he should go the top of Pisgah, and lift his eyes in all the four directions and see the land with his eyes. (cf. Numbers 20:8-10; Deuteronomy 3:21-29; 1 Corinthians 10:4, 6)

However, Moses appeared to Peter, James and his brother John at the transfiguration of Lord Jesus and it shows that Moses is in heaven. We have, therefore, enough reason to believe that he will come as one of the two witnesses and bear testimony for the Lord thus completing his unfinished assignment.

# CHAPTER 34
# OUR HAIR ARE NUMBERED

But the very hairs of your head are all numbered. (Matthew 10:30)

Is it not wonderful that our God knows us not only by our names but by every detail that is in us including the number of hairs on our head. He has count of them and yet we stumble in faith several times. It is our weakness that we fail to understand the mighty power of God and his provision for us. However, we should be aware of the fact that if we neglect or doubt his care for us we will reap the consequences of our disbelief and run into loss.

The children of Israel stumbled upon their faith in the Lord and paid severely for their lack of faith. They feared that the giants whom their representatives saw were capable of harming them whereas God said no weapon formed against them will prosper. Every one of the age above twenty years including Moses and Aaron, except Joshua and Caleb, died before they reached the Promised Land of Canaan. The details are in Numbers chapter 14

On hearing the evil report from the ten spies the congregation cried whole night and murmured against Moses and Aaron. The congregation asked Moses and Aaron if God wanted them to die in the wilderness and asked why they were moved out of Egypt with the promise that they would have a better life!

After hearing the evil report from the ten the children of Israel preferred to go back to slavery in Egypt rather than die in the wilderness. This was their disappointment because of their lack of faith in God who promised them the land flowing with milk and honey.

This was the result of their lack of belief in God who gave them protection from rain and heat. They never lacked food, nor did their shoe wear out during their entire journey for forty years.

However, they believed the discouraging evil report of the ten men who went out to make a survey of the land. They sent their emissaries to make their own choice despite God's promise that he would bless them with land that had abundance. Their own witnesses brought a cluster of grapes hanging on a staff carried by two men from that land to them to see, yet when they heard that there were Anakites, who were giants they lost faith.

Perhaps, they thought their God was smaller than the giants their men saw in the land. The men felt that they were like grasshoppers before the giants in spite of the fact that they defeated mighty kings on their journey with the help of God.

Now that the children of Israelites were entrapped in their own false beliefs and lack of faith in God, they forged forward to kill Moses and Aaron, who were interceding on behalf of them to God all through their journey.

The children of Israel were making a decision to choose a captain to lead them back to Egypt from where they came to Kadeshbarnea, which was so close to the Promised Land. They wanted to go back from blessings to curse and lead a life of slavery in a sinful land once again.

Earlier, when they were in Egypt crying to God for help and prayed that they may be delivered from the slavery, God heard their cry and redeemed them from the bondage of slavery under Pharaoh.

Until God executed the last plague of killing the firstborn of Egyptians, Pharaoh did not allow them to leave Egypt. Israelites saw that their own firstborn were spared by God, yet now listening to disappointing evil report they changed their mind. How feeble and frail was their mind that they lost faith in their God and believed in the evil report.

Moses, who interceded on their behalf several times, fell once again face down before the congregation of all the children of Israel to cry to the Lord. Aaron accompanied Moses in his prayers and Joshua and Caleb tore down their clothes to support Moses and Aaron.

God heard their prayer and promised them pardon yet their earthly blessings of possessing the land of Canaan were lost to them in their time. That land which was with milk and honey flowing was promised to them for their possession but all those who started their journey from Egypt, except Joshua and Caleb and those who were below the age of twenty years, perished in the wilderness.

If you are not yet saved this is the day for accepting Jesus as your personal savior. Do not fear any adversity. You are of more value than many sparrows, who toil not, yet they have their food and protection every day.

If you are saved already, then never fear those who have the authority over your flesh but fear the one who has the authority over body, soul and spirit. Jesus said he has overcome this world. He is Lord Jesus Christ who is the only savior. Salvation of a believer is never lost, yet believer should live a holy life always.

"Fear ye not therefore, ye are of more value than many sparrows. Whosoever therefore shall confess me before men, him will I confess also before my Father which is in heaven" (Matthew 10:31-32)

# CHATER 35
# POOR PROTECTED

"For whosoever shall give you a cup of water to drink in my name, because ye belong to Christ, verily I say unto you, he shall not lose his reward. And whosoever shall offend one of these little ones that believe in me, it is better for him that a millstone were hanged about his neck, and he were cast into the sea. And if thy hand offend thee, cut it off: it is better for thee to enter into life maimed, than having two hands to go into hell, into the fire that never shall be quenched: Where their worm dieth not, and the fire is not quenched". (Mark 9:41-44)

Taking cue from the happenings among the children of Israel we can understand the ways of God and how he detested idolatry, idolaters and those who offend the children of God.

King Jeroboam's scheme of misguiding and misleading the "House of Israel" did not end at making two calves of gold for them and saying that those were the gods who brought them out of Egypt, but he set one of the golden calves at "Bethel" on the border between Northern Kingdom and Southern Kingdom and another golden calf at "Dan" which was the Northern border of his kingdom. He was successful in misleading his people to be in his kingdom and worship the idols at Dan and Bethel rather than they go to Jerusalem to celebrate Passover festival on fifteenth day of the eighth month.

Jeroboam took the lead in worshipping the idols and burning incense to them. Once Jeroboam was standing at the altar at Bethel to worship the idol and burn incense to it when a man of God from Judah went there according to the word of the LORD and prophesied saying:

"...O altar, altar, thus saith the LORD; Behold, a child shall be born unto the house of David, Josiah by name; and upon thee shall he offer the priests of the high places that burn incense upon thee, and men's bones shall be burnt upon thee". The prophet also said that that the altar will be rent and the ashes there on the altar shall be poured out. (Ref. 1 Kings 13:2, 3)

The prophecy of the man of God was fulfilled during king Josiah's reign. Josiah was eight years old when he took over as king of Judah and he reigned for thirty one years. He was one of the rarest kings who did that which was right in the sight of the LORD. At the orders of king Josiah, Hilkiah the high priest of the second order, and door-keepers brought all the vessels that were made for Baal, and for the grove, and all the host of heaven and burnt them and carried their ashes to Bethel. Even before the division of the unified Kingdom of Israel occurred the idolatry had its way into the kingdom ruled by Solomon. Josiah like his great grandfather Hezekiah removed idolatry from his kingdom. The sin increases in the land when its rulers are themselves encourage it and they all face the consequences. The LORD is pleased with those who walk in His ways and Josiah was one who did that which was right in the sight of the LORD and it pleased the LORD.

During the reign of Josiah there were priests in his kingdom who ordained to burn incense in the high places of Judah, and to the entire host in heaven, and in the places round about Jerusalem. Josiah removed all the priests from their positions.

Josiah looked around and got the human bones removed from the sepulchers and burned them upon the altar and thus desecrating it. It was according to the word of the LORD spoken by the man of God as we read in 1 Kings 13:2. When

Josiah saw a sepulcher that was distinct from the others he inquired about it and the people said it was the sepulcher of the man of God who came from Judah and prophesied about burning of human bones on the altar at Bethel, the very thing that he did there. Then, Josiah ordered that the sepulcher of the man of God may not be exhumed to take out his bones. In addition, Josiah also removed all shrines at the high places that the king of Israel built in Samaria and slaughtered all the priests upon the altars and burnt the human bones on them and went back to Jerusalem.

Josiah ordered to celebrate Passover festival. It was first time the Passover festival was celebrated at Jerusalem since the time when Judges ruled Israel even up to eighteenth year of his reign. (cf. 1 Kings Ch. 13 and 2 Kings Ch. 23)

Jesus speaking to his disciples said whoever gives them a cup of water to drink in His name, because they belong to Him, shall surely receive his/her reward. The Lord was very shrewd in saying that it is better for those who offend one of the little ones that believe in Him to have a millstone hang around his neck and be into the sea. He said it is better to cut off the part of the body that offends rather than allowing whole body perishing in the lake of fire (Ref. Mark 9:41-44)

Such Kings and authorities of the like that of King Jeroboam who offend the children of God offering worship to the living God will have their day to be surely reckoned with those who will be cast in the lake of fire.

# CHAPTER 36
# ALL FOR GOOD

*"And we know that all things work together for good to them that love God, to them who are the called according to his purpose"* *(Romans 8:28)*

And Joseph said unto them, Fear not: for am I in the place of God? But as for you, ye thought evil against me; but God meant it unto good, to bring to pass, as it is this day, to save much people alive. Now therefore fear ye not: I will nourish you, and your little ones. And he comforted them, and spake kindly unto them" (Genesis 50:19-21)

Nothing that happens in our lives happens without the knowledge of God. Although the world belongs to Satan, the Lord God is Almighty and He controls everything in this world rendering Satan's works ineffective in the lives of those who are chosen by Him, and are called according to His purpose. The Lord gives us victory over Satan when we depend on Him.

Joseph was sold into Egypt and later from a very humble position he was elevated as Governor of the land; next only to Pharaoh in the land of Egypt. He was in charge of distribution of food in Egypt during the seven-year famine in Canaan.

Joseph's early life was pathetic and filled with sorrows, and it appears as if God was not with him, but his later life proves that it was not so.

He was loved greatly by Jacob his father but his brothers envied him and threw him into waterless cistern from where he was pulled out and was sold to Midianites.

As the time passed by he was thrown into prison on false accusation leveled against him by Potiphar's wife, who seduced him into having illicit relationship with her, when her husband was away. Joseph refused her request and consequently he had to face the wrath of Potiphar, who was taken away by his wife's lies. On this cause Joseph suffered imprisonment for two years.

However, God was with Joseph, who was on the only one given intelligence by God to interpret two tough dreams of Pharaoh. The Pharaoh was pleased with Joseph's interpretations of his dreams and ordered not only his release from the prison but made him Governor of the land.

"And Pharaoh said unto Joseph, I am Pharaoh, and without thee shall no man lift up his hand or foot in all the land of Egypt" (Genesis 41:44)

"And Joseph was the governor over the land, and he it was that sold to all the people of the land: and Joseph's brethren came, and bowed down themselves before him with their faces to the earth" (Genesis 42:6)

Joseph's brothers were sent by Jacob to Egypt to fetch food for them and later Jacob and all of Joseph's brothers settled in Egypt at the behest of Joseph. Jacob was reluctant to go to Egypt but God assured him that He will bring them back into the Promised Land.

"And he said, I am God, the God of thy father: fear not to go down into Egypt; for I will there make of thee a great nation: I will go down with thee into Egypt; and I will also surely bring thee up again: and Joseph shall put his hand upon thine eyes. And Jacob rose up from Beersheba: and the sons of Israel carried Jacob their father, and their little ones, and their wives, in the wagons which Pharaoh had sent to carry him" (Genesis 46:3-5)

When Joseph's brothers fell prostrate before Joseph seeking food, Joseph went aside and wept for them. Also, Jacob bowed down to Joseph, none of them knowing that He was Joseph. One of the dreams of Joseph was fulfilled in its entirety but the second one was fulfilled only partially. Jacob's wife Rachel was already dead when Joseph had his dreams.

"And Rachel died, and was buried in the way to Ephrath, which is Bethlehem" (Genesis 35:19)

Joseph's other dream came true. (cf. Genesis 37:5-8; 37:9-11). The unfulfilled dream of Rachel bowing down to Joseph will be fulfilled in the Kingdom of God, when Lord Jesus returns and brings with Him all that were dead in Him and were raised. (cf. 1 Thessalonians 4:13-16).

"For if we believe that Jesus died and rose again, even so them also which sleep in Jesus will God bring with him" (1 Thessalonians 4:14)

After the death of Jacob, Joseph's brothers were so fearful that they said among themselves that Joseph would hate them, and will surely requite them the evil that they did to him before he was sold into Egypt. With that fear in their mind they sent a messenger to Joseph seeking, on behalf of them, forgiveness saying their father was dead. In order that they may find favor in the sight of Joseph the brothers did not hesitate to identify that they were servants of the God of Joseph's father Jacob.

Joseph's brothers also went with the messenger and they fell down before Joseph's face and said "Behold, we by thy servants". It is at that time that Joseph said to his brothers...

"And his brethren also went and fell down before his face; and they said, Behold, we be thy servants. And Joseph said unto them, Fear not: for am I in the place of God? But as for you, ye thought evil against me; but God meant it unto good, to bring to pass, as it is this day, to save much people alive" (Genesis 50:18-20)

Joseph, who was the Governor and in charge of distribution of food in Egypt, during severe famine in the land of Canaan, could have retorted and requited them of their evil done to him, but contrary to their fears they saw Joseph acknowledging God love and providence.

Joseph said to them, "Fear not: for am I in the place of God? But as for you, ye thought evil against me; but God meant it unto good, to bring to pass, as it is this day, to save much people alive"

Although circumstances were adverse for Joseph in the beginning, he was the one chosen by God to help his brothers and parents in miraculous way. He forgave his brothers of all their trespasses against him, and said they intended it for bad but God meant it for good for not only Joseph but to his entire family.

Let us also realize that in all our adverse situations God will be us and never leaves us. He says "fear not". We may peradventure think that everything is going wrong for us, but only time will tell that God was preparing a blessed situation for us. Everything works for good for those who love God and who are called according to His purpose.

# CHAPTER 37
# HEIR OF ALL THINGS

"Who being the brightness of his glory, and the express image of his person, and upholding all things by the word of his power, when he had by himself purged our sins, sat down on the right hand of the Majesty on high" (Hebrews 1:3)

There is narration in Genesis Chapter 1 of whole creation that was created by God. He created heavens, earth and everything in the heavens, in the earth, and in the seas by His Word. He created them out of nothing. The whole creation came into existence out of nothing and in obedience to the LORD's Word.

God said, "Let there be light: and there was light". God said "Let there be firmament in the midst of the waters" and it was so. He said let it divide the waters from waters" and it was so. He said "let there be" and it was!

Evolution theory has flaws, and Big Bang Theory has flaws but God's Word stands forever and ever. This amazing creation of God is held together by the power of the Word of Lord Jesus Christ, who purged our sins and sat down at the right of the Majesty on high. He is pleading on our behalf while the adversary is continuously accusing us before the LORD.

Job never cursed God in spite of facing huge losses and suffering sickness; however like any man getting disappointed in adverse situations, he was also dejected and yet did not question the Almighty God as to what the LORD was doing in his life. Job faced trials and tribulations, of great magnitude. Not a single person on this earth faced so great trials and tribulations from the creation until now.

It is interesting to note that God never proved His existence to any human being; rather He left enough evidence for mankind to seek Him and find Him. Man tries to prove God's existence and non-existence, and finally believe if not in God, in something else, and worships if not in God, in something else.

Many a man worships now God's creation instead of the Creator. Finally, there will come a time when man, who does not seek to worship God, choses to worship Antichrist. Thus man prefers to worship man rather than God.

Even an atheist, who says he does not believe in anything, finally believes in something, and worships something other than true God. He finally ends up nowhere groping in darkness depicting his lack of hope of his future life after his death.

The LORD answered Job out of whirlwind and asked several questions that perplexed Job, who finally gave up to God and said he would rather shut his mouth than answer any question from the LORD.

'Who is this that hides counsel without knowledge?' Therefore I have uttered what I did not understand, things too wonderful for me, which I did not know. 'Hear, and I will speak; I will question you, and you make it known to me.'

I had heard of you by the hearing of the ear, but now my eye sees you; therefore I despise myself, and repent in dust and ashes." (Job 42:3-6 ESV)

This is the LORD Jehovah, who made Lord Jesus Christ the heir of all things, by whom also He made the worlds. Lord Jesus is the brightness of Jehovah's glory and express image of His person. He is upholding all things by the word of His power (Ref. Hebrews 1:1-3)

John describes Lord Jesus Christ that He was eternally with the Father. The Word was made flesh and lived among us. Paul writes that He came into this world in the form of a servant in the likeness of man (Ref. John 1:1-18; Philippians 2:6-9)

".who, though he was in the form of God, did not count equality with God a thing to be grasped, but emptied himself, by taking the form of a servant, being born in the likeness of men. And being found in human form, he humbled himself by becoming obedient to the point of death, even death on a cross. Therefore God has highly exalted him and bestowed on him the name that is above every name, so that at the name of Jesus every knee should bow, in heaven and on earth and under the earth, and every tongue confess that Jesus Christ is Lord, to the glory of God the Father" (Philippians 2:6-11 ESV)

Jesus died on the cross for our sins and paid the price for our salvation. There is salvation in Him and Him alone. He forgives us all our sins if we confess our sins to Him and accept Him as Lord, and believe in heart that God raised Him from the dead. (Ref. Romans 10:9)

# CHAPTER 38
# A BETER COVENANT

*"For what the law could not do, in that it was weak through the flesh, God sending his own Son in the likeness of sinful flesh, and for sin, condemned sin in the flesh" (Romans 8:3)*

Seated on the right hand of the throne of the Majesty In heavens is our Lord Jesus Christ, who is our high priest pleading our behalf. In heavens is the true tabernacle which the Lord pitched and not man. In that tabernacle is the Lord Jesus Christ, who is the true minister of the Sanctuary.

In the Old Testament period every high priest was ordained to offer sacrifices and oblations, which were examples of the things to come, while in the New Testament period Lord Jesus Christ had to offer an excellent sacrifices and oblation of His own body and blood.

The priests of the Aaronic order from the Levite tribe offered sacrifices and oblations according to the Law of Moses as given by God as shadows and those shadows were fulfilled in the substance. Those things that were to come were the body and the blood of Lord Jesus Christ.

Lord Jesus who was not an earthly priest, but the Son of God, from above, of the order of Melchisedec, did not offer such earthly sacrifices and oblations, as priests of Aaronic order offered, but offered His body and blood as the Son of God on behalf of us.

Just as every high priest of the order of Aaron offered gifts and sacrifices for covering sin of himself first and then of all the children of Israel, it was necessary for Lord Jesus Christ to offer His body and blood once and for all for the remission of our sins. The covering of the sin in the Old Testament period was not sufficient to fully remove the Sin from the one who was seeking forgiveness, but only covered it temporarily until that Sin was fully removed by the precious blood of Lord Jesus Christ.

Moses was divinely instructed by the LORD, on the Mount Sinai, of the pattern of the tabernacle; however, Lord Jesus Christ had obtained an excellent ministry better than the old one, by entering into heavenly sanctuary with his own blood. He is the mediator of better covenant that was established on better promises. The Old Covenant had shortcomings inasmuch as, all that was done concerning offering of sacrifices and oblations, they were in the form of shadows of the real substance that was to come (cf. Hebrews 8:1-7).

A better covenant was, therefore, necessary, and the prophecy spoken in Jer. 31:33-34 is fulfilled.

*"But this shall be the covenant that I will make with the house of Israel; after those days, saith the LORD, I will put my law in their inward parts, and write it in their hearts; and will be their God, and they shall be my people. And they shall teach no more every man his neighbour, and every man his brother, saying, Know the LORD: for they shall all know me, from the least of them unto the greatest of them, saith the LORD: for I will forgive their iniquity, and I will remember their sin no more" (Jeremiah 31:33-34)*

A better covenant was in replacement of it with a New Covenant. It is not according to the one that God made with the patriarchs on the day when He took them by His hand and led them out of slavery under Pharaoh in Egypt.

The Old Covenant demanded from the children of Israel their compliance of God's Laws and Statutes failing which they would lose God's blessings. Their blessings were dependent on the conditions imposed by God, unlike Abrahamic Covenant which was unconditional.

The phrase "if you will" as we read in Exodus 19:5 was very much part of their receiving the blessings, unlike the phrase "I will" as we read in Hebrews 8:10, 12.

*"Not according to the covenant that I made with their fathers in the day when I took them by the hand to lead them out of the land of Egypt; because they continued not in my covenant, and I regarded them not, saith the Lord. For this is the covenant that I will make with the house of Israel after those days, saith the Lord; I will put my laws into their mind, and write them in their hearts: and I will be to them a God, and they shall be to me a people: And they shall not teach every man his neighbour, and every man his brother, saying, Know the Lord: for all shall know me, from the least to the greatest. For I will be merciful to their unrighteousness, and their sins and their iniquities will I remember no more" (Hebrews 8:9-12)*

The Old Covenant demanded obedience out of fear as against the New Covenant which demanded a willing heart and God's promise that He will not remember repentant individuals any more. (cf. Hebrews 2:2; 12:25-27; 8:10; 10:17)

Even though Aaron was the high priest God said to him through Moses not to enter the "Holy place" as and when he wants to, but enter only as and when God wants him to (cf. Lev.16:2), whereas Christians, who are saved by grace through faith, according to the provisions of New Testament pattern have free access to God through Lord Jesus Christ, the only mediator (cf. Ephesians 2:8, 18)

Lord Jesus Christ made the New Covenant in His blood that was shed on the cross.

*"And he took bread, and when he had given thanks, he broke it and gave it to them, saying, "This is my body, which is given for you. Do this in remembrance of me." 20 And likewise the cup after they had eaten, saying, "This cup that is poured out for you is the new covenant in my blood""" (Luke 22:19-20 ESV)*

*"For there is one God, and one mediator between God and men, the man Christ Jesus" (1 Timothy 2:5)*

*"For on the one hand, a former commandment is set aside because of its weakness and uselessness 19 (for the law made nothing perfect); but on the other hand, a better hope is introduced, through which we draw near to God" (Hebrews 7:18, 19 ESV)*

*"For what the law could not do, in that it was weak through the flesh, God sending his own Son in the likeness of sinful flesh, and for sin, condemned sin in the flesh: That the righteousness of the law might be fulfilled in us, who walk not after the flesh, but after the Spirit" (Romans 8:3-4)*

If so, was there an error in establishing Old Covenant first and then the New Covenant? No, that was the way the children of Israel were needed to be taught. They lived a slavery life and their life needed to be built gradually. Even after entering into the Promised Land God did not remove their enemies overnight, but removed them gradually. God has undying love for the children of Israel and that is why the Scriptures say in

Romans Chapter 11 that God has not castaway them, but has blinded their understanding for a period of time in order to bring Gentiles into salvation.

Apostle Paul describes such an arrangement as...

*"Wherefore the law was our schoolmaster to bring us unto Christ, that we might be justified by faith. But after that faith is come, we are no longer under a schoolmaster" (Galatians 3:24-25).*

# CHAPTER 39
# ROYAL PRIESTHOOD

*"But ye are a chosen generation, a royal priesthood, an holy nation, a peculiar people; that ye should shew forth the praises of him who hath called you out of darkness into his marvellous light"* (1 Peter 2:9)

1 Peter 2:9 lists the position of believers in the sight of our living God. Believers in Christ are a chosen generation, a royal priesthood, an holy nation, a peculiar people and then it lists the responsibilities of believer towards the One who has given such status before him. God called us from out of darkness into marvelous light in order that we may worship him, praise him and bear a good testimony for him.

The priests in the Old Testament period were required to offer sacrifices for themselves and then for the congregation which they were heading. It differed as the times changed and the way they offered sacrifices varied in different time periods.

Until the Mosaic Law came into existence individual saints in the Old Testament offered Sacrifices all by themselves that entitled them to be called as priests; and after the Law was proposed the entire congregations of the children of Israel were called the "Kingdom of Priests", but because they violated the Law the priestly office was confined to the tribe of Levi. Aaron and his sons became the priests. The high priest could enter the Most Holy Place in the Tabernacle only once a year on the 'Day of Atonement'.

There are at least four individuals who can be taken for consideration. (1) Noah (2) Abraham (3) Isaac and (4) Jacob

Noah built an altar unto the Lord and offered clean beast, and clean fowl as burnt offerings on the altar. (Genesis 8:20) Abraham took two of his young men with him and Isaac his son and went to offer the burnt offering. (Genesis 22:3). Isaac built an altar and called upon the name of the Lord, and pitched his tent and his servants digged a well (Genesis 26:25). Jacob offered sacrifice upon the mount and called his brothers to eat bread and they ate the bread. (Genesis 31:54)

Then after the Law was proposed the children of Israel as a whole nation was called "kingdom of priests" (Exodus 19:6) But they violated the Law and antagonized God several times. They worshipped Idols and angered God. Then, God confined priesthood to the Tribe of Levi. Aaron and his sons from the Tribe of Levi were the priests. (Exodus 28:1)

"And hath made us kings and priests unto God and his Father; to him be glory and dominion for ever and ever. Amen". (Revelation 1:6) This shows the priesthood of individual believers in the present age.

The sons of Aaron were anointed. They had on them Ephod, which is a linen apron, bonnet, which is a cap, breastplate, which is a metal piece worn around the body as a defensive armor, and mitre which is a head-band used as a turban. The stipulations God prescribed for priests were so stringent that they could not violate any of the conditions that God prescribed. These details are mentioned in Exodus Ch. 27, 28 and 29

Lord Jesus Christ was not after the order of Aaron but he was after the order of Melchizedek. While the priesthood of Aaron was limited; the priesthood of Melchizedek is for ever and ever. Even though there are not many references about Melchizedek, yet the references that are found in Genesis 14:18, Psalm 110:4, Hebrews 5:6 and in Hebrews Chapter 7 give us great knowledge about Lord Jesus Christ's Priesthood after the order of Melchizedek. Jesus is Priest, Prophet and King. Jesus became our High Priest because he offered himself as a sacrifice for our sins.

*"For every high priest taken from among men is ordained for men in things pertaining to God, that he may offer both gifts and sacrifices for sins" (Hebrews 5:1)*

*"But into the second went the high priest alone once every year, not without blood, which he offered for himself, and for the errors of the people" (Hebrews 9:7)*

*"By a new and living way, which he hath consecrated for us, through the veil, that is to say, his flesh" (Hebrews 10:20)*

Having therefore, brethren, boldness to enter into the holiest by the blood of Jesus, By a new and living way, which he hath consecrated for us, through the veil, that is to say, his flesh; And having an high priest over the house of God; Let us draw near with a true heart in full assurance of faith, having our hearts sprinkled from an evil conscience, and our bodies washed with pure water. (Hebrews 10:19-22)

According to Levite priesthood a priest could not be king and likewise a King could not be a priest. That is the reason why we see King Saul was not accepted by God as priest.

"And Saul said, Bring hither a burnt offering to me, and peace offerings. And he offered the burnt offering". (1 Samuel 13:9)

The result was seen in 1 Samuel 13:13

"And Samuel said to Saul, Thou hast done foolishly: thou hast not kept the commandment of the LORD thy God, which he commanded thee: for now would the LORD have established thy kingdom upon Israel for ever". (1 Samuel 13:13)

Melchizedek king of Salem was not of the order of Levites. Abraham gave him tithe to Melchizedek.

"And Melchizedek king of Salem brought forth bread and wine: and he was the priest of the most high God. And he blessed him, and said, Blessed be Abram of the most high God, possessor of heaven and earth: And blessed be the most high God, which hath delivered thine enemies into thy hand. And he gave him tithes of all". (Genesis 14:18-20)

"For this Melchisedec, king of Salem, priest of the most high God, who met Abraham returning from the slaughter of the kings, and blessed him" (Hebrews 7:1)

When Jesus was crucified the veil in the temple was rent into two from top to bottom signifying granting to us access to the Father through the Son of God, who is our High Priest. There is, therefore, no more a Priest required for us to offer sacrifices on our behalf nor are we required to confess our sins to any Priest in this world in order that he may convey to God our sins to be forgiven. We are all priests and he has given us the status of "Royal Priesthood" and Lord Jesus Christ is our High Priest and mediator. (Matthew 27:51)

"But Christ being come an high priest of good things to come, by a greater and more perfect tabernacle, not made with hands, that is to say, not of this building" (Hebrews 9:11)

We are given responsibility to offer sacrifices and those sacrifices are presenting our bodies as living sacrifice, holy and acceptable unto God. (Romans 12:1). We should be ready to help our brethren (1 John 3:16). We should visit the fatherless and widows in their affliction, and keep ourselves without any blemish. (James 1:27). We should offer sacrifices of praises and thanks to God continually. (Hebrews 13:15)

"I exhort therefore, that, first of all, supplications, prayers, intercessions, and giving of thanks, be made for all men"(1 Timothy 2:1)

# CHAPTER 40
# LIVING SACRIFICE

*"I appeal to you therefore, brothers, by the mercies of God, to present your bodies as a living sacrifice, holy and acceptable to God, which is your spiritual worship. Do not be conformed to this world, but be transformed by the renewal of your mind, that by testing you may discern what is the will of God, what is good and acceptable and perfect" (Romans 12:1-3 ESV)*

Apostle Paul uses a unique word, 'beseech' while addressing Chief Captain (Acts 21:39), King Agrippa (Acts 26:3), brethren at Rome (Romans 12:1 and 15:30) brethren at Corinthians (1 Cor.1:10), which shows how loving and humble he was in his approach with others. 'Beseech' means to beg anxiously, or to request earnestly.

In this verse Paul requests earnestly his fellow believers at Rome to present their bodies a living sacrifice. What exactly 'living sacrifice' means?

In the Old Testament period, the physical sacrifices are made to God to have reconciliation with him by way of 'Atonement' for the sin man had committed. The sacrifices could be a goat, a lamb, or turtledoves.

Inasmuch as Christ became our 'propitiation', we in this New Testament period are no longer required to offer the physical offerings. Christ's blood that was shed and His body that bore our sins is enough for salvation.

All that an unbeliever has to do is to believe this fact, confess his/her sins to Lord Jesus, and accept him as "Lord" and believe in heart that God raised Him from the dead. After that we continually offer our bodies as living sacrifice unto God.

The believers in Christ are to show kindness, humbleness of mind, meekness, and longsuffering (Col. 3:12), present bodies as holy temple because the Spirit of God lives in us (1 Corinthians 3:16), and worship him in truth and sprit. This is the reasonable service unto him.

The true worship is not a forced one, but of voluntary and it emanates from the bottom of heart, offering ourselves fully unto him with complete devotion.

*"Know ye not that ye are the temple of God, and that the Spirit of God dwelleth in you?" (1 Corinthians 3:16)*

www.ingramcontent.com/pod-product-compliance
Lightning Source LLC
Chambersburg PA
CBHW060755050426
42449CB00008B/1417